BRAHMS
his life and times

BRAHMS

his life and times

Paul Holmes

The Baton Press

To my father and in
memory of my mother

Midas Life and Times of the Great Composers

BACH	Tim Dowley
BARTOK	Hamish Milne
BEETHOVEN	Ateş Orga
BERLIOZ	Robert Clarson-Leach
BRAHMS	Paul Holmes
CHOPIN	Ateş Orga
DVORAK	Neil Butterworth
ELGAR	Simon Mundy
HAYDN	Neil Butterworth
LISZT	Bryce Morrison
MAHLER	Edward Seckerson
MENDELSSOHN	Mozelle Moshansky
MOZART	Peggy Woodford
OFFENBACH	Peter Gammond
PROKOFIEV	David Gutman
RACHMANINOFF	Robert Walker
RAVEL	Burnett James
ROSSINI	Nicholas Till
SCHUBERT	Peggy Woodford
SCHUMANN	Tim Dowley
SHOSTAKOVICH	Eric Roseberry
TCHAIKOVSKY	Wilson Strutte
VERDI	Peter Southwell-Sander

Other Baton Press Music Titles

John Ireland	Muriel Searle
Double Life	Miklos Rozsa
Wagner	David Burnett James
Paganini	John Sugden
The Strauss Family	Peter Kemp

© Paul Holmes 1984

First published in UK in 1984 by
THE BATON PRESS
44 Holden Park Road,
Southborough, Kent TN4 OER

ISBN 0 85936 146 2

First published in USA in 1984 by
HIPPOCRENE BOOKS
171 Madison Avenue, New York, NY 10016

ISBN 0 88254 728 3

Printed in Great Britain by
The Pitman Press, Bath

Contents

Acknowledgements

I would like to thank Mike Fenton and John Evans for their help and encouragement during the writing of this book. I would also like to thank the British Institute of Recorded Sound for allowing me to hear the voice of Brahms.

I must thank the following publishers for their permission to include extracts from letters and journals:– Edward Arnold – The Letters of Clara Schumann and Johannes Brahms, ed. Berthold Litzmann; John Murray – The Herzogenberg Correspondence; George Allen and Unwin – Brahms, his Life and Works by Karl Geiringer.

Illustrations on pages 11 (lower), 14, 18, 20, 22, 23, 28, 33, 36–7, 38, 52, 55, 56, 73, 76, 77, 95, 103, 104, 137, 138, 141, 146 and 148 were supplied by, and reproduced with the kind permission of, The Mary Evans Picture Library, London.

Illustrations on pages 63, 67, 90 and 132 were supplied by, and reproduced with the kind permission of, The Mansell Collection, London.

Illustrations on pages 60, 96 were supplied by, and reproduced with the kind permission of, The Radio Times Hulton Picture Library, London.

Illustration on page 97 supplied by, and reproduced with the kind permission of, The National Portrait Gallery, London.

1 Squalor

On leaving a gathering of friends, the elderly Brahms turned to his devastated hostess and said: 'If there is anyone here whom I have not yet insulted, please give him my compliments!' He then stormed off to spend the rest of the evening drinking in his favourite restaurant.

Photographs of the period show him as gruff and bearded, gazing coldly and uncompromisingly at the onlooker, about to bark out another of the withering sarcasms that became his social speciality in later years. Yet by this time he had written a lyrically tender violin concerto, was extravagantly, although always anonymously, generous with money, and gave hours of his time to nurture genuine talent with no hope of material reward.

The key to such a man's character must always be something of a mystery, and he made sure that he covered his tracks. A repressed romantic, a deeply emotional man held back by social disadvantage and an innate shyness, an intellectual at odds with a passionate soul – Brahms was all of these. If he eventually shrank from any attempt to discuss his emotions, he continued to play out the drama of his inner life behind the mask of abstract music.

He was born in the slums of Hamburg on 7 May 1833. Beethoven, who was to cast such a long shadow over the mature man, had been dead for six years; Schubert, whom he revered almost as much, for five. Among those composers who were to influence his life directly, Wagner, aged twenty, had only just embarked on his first, soon forgotten opera, and Liszt, aged twenty-two, already a virtuoso pianist, was beginning the first of his great love affairs, while Schumann, also twenty-two, had barely tried his wings. The Romantic age in art was virtually over and the nation cradling the new-born composer could not even be said to exist. As heir to the long-defunct Holy Roman Empire, it included over a hundred autonomous and semi-autonomous political units. Besides kingdoms like Prussia, Bavaria and Hanover, there were dozens of dukedoms, principalities and states no larger than a city.

Hamburg was just such a political entity – a rich free port on the River Elbe, wedged between the Kingdom of Hanover and the disputed province of Schleswig-Holstein, but with a tradition of proud independence harking back to its membership of the Hanseatic merchants' league. It was an ancient city as well as a bustling modern port, at once entirely cosmopolitan and entirely provincial. Great churches, merchants' houses and guildhalls embodied the public face of its smugly isolated wealth, but its fine thoroughfares ran down through narrow, cobbled alleyways and lightless courts to a tangle of close-packed, rat-infested houses near the harbours, where the elegant burghers did not stray. Bars and brothels catered for all the tastes of all the nations of the earth, and it was there in the Gängviertel, or Lane Quarter, an area nicknamed 'Adulterers' Walk', that Johannes Brahms spent the first twenty years of his life.

Yet although his surroundings were squalid, he was blessed with devoted and respectable parents who struggled hard to rise above their circumstances. His father, Johann Jakob Brahms, was the son of a Holstein innkeeper. Despite parental opposition, he had decided to become a musician, had taught himself to play all the stringed instruments, plus the flute and French horn, and had then left home at the age of nineteen to make his career in Hamburg. At first, the only work he could find was playing in the Gängviertel bars for a subsistence wage until he joined a newly formed musicians' guild that provided him with contacts as well as a measure of social life. Practicality forced him to play the double bass regularly, but with this unglamorous skill he eventually joined a sextet playing in the fashionable Alster Pavilion gardens. As a member of the Hamburg militia, he also achieved some status as an *oberjäger*. Brahms told Clara Schumann many years later: 'I was not a *citizen* of Hamburg but the son of a burgher of that town.' From there, he hoped to climb higher, and moved to slightly better lodgings. There he met his future wife, Christiane Nissen, the sister-in-law of his landlord. As Christiane wrote to Johannes many years later:

He had barely been living with us a week when he wanted me to become his wife. I could hardly believe it, because our ages were so different.

Their whirlwind courtship was not exactly the stuff of romantic fiction, for Christiane was forty-one, had one leg shorter than the other and was extremely plain, whereas Jakob was only twenty-four, a good-looking man in the pink of health.

But Christiane was, by all accounts, a highly practical and positive woman with some education and literate to a high degree, as her correspondence with Johannes was to show. She was also descended from a minor branch of German aristocracy, although she had been reduced to working as a seamstress and servant as well as helping in a haberdashery shop before meeting Jakob. Her virtues must have weighed heavily against her physical disadvantages so Jakob Brahms probably made a conscious choice for practicality and a measure of social status over the chancy business of a love match with someone closer his own age.

Whatever the reasons, they appear to have been only superficially mismatched. Both delighted in life and could turn

The house where Brahms was born. Florence May, visiting it seventy years later, wrote: 'On entering it, it is difficult to repress a shiver of bewilderment and dismay.' The house was destroyed during an air raid in 1943.

Jakob Brahms in 1838.

Brahms's mother towards the end of her life.

Elise Brahms in 1860.

the smallest pleasures into sources of joy. Such a disposition was sorely needed in the slumland apartment to which they now moved, and where they were to spend the first few years of their married life. Seventy years later, Florence May, who came to know Johannes Brahms well, visited it and left a vivid account of its squalor:

It stands in a small, dismal court . . . a steep wooden staircase leads . . . to the various stories of the building . . . On entering it, it is difficult to repress a shiver of bewilderment and dismay. The staircase door opens onto a diminutive space, half kitchen, half lobby where some cooking may be done and a child's bed made up, and which has a second door leading to the living room. This communicates with the sleeping closet, which has its own window, but it is so tiny it can scarcely be called a room. There is nothing else, neither corner nor cupboard.

Christiane made the dingy rooms as bright and cheerful as she could with caged birds, plants and colourful fabrics, then they started a family. First a daughter, Elise, in 1831, and two years after Johannes was born, another son, Fritz. At this point, the family found a larger apartment and Christiane was able to open a small haberdashers to supplement her husband's erratic wages.

Johannes' first impressions were strongly coloured by the sounds of music and he claimed to have invented a system of musical notation before he was five. However, it was not one of the instruments that his father played that interested him, but the piano, which he heard on visits to members of his father's guild. With something of Jakob's stubbornness therefore, he rejected his father's attempts to make him learn an orchestral instrument with a view, no doubt, to his making a living as an all-round musician, and demanded to learn the piano instead.

Although this was the age of the virtuoso pianist, with Liszt, Chopin and Kalkbrenner making vast sums of money and commanding wild adulation, the training was too specialised for someone with untried talents, and even if Johannes did establish himself, the career was often precarious and short. Jakob compromised, and sent his son at the age of seven to study with Friedrich Cossel – a highly respected, although impoverished, pianist and a sound musician in Jakob's circle who could be relied on to give the child a thorough training in all branches of music. There was no favouritism, either, for Fritz Brahms was also sent to Cossel when he was old enough, and both brothers attended the same primary school where they received an excellent, although unfashionable, education. Only Elise, as the girl, was excluded, but her predilection for migraine had much to do with this. It was not easy to pay for such expert tuition on Jakob's small salary, but he felt justified when Cossel reported that Johannes had the makings of a gifted and, above all, an original musician.

Johannes was diligent and worked hard. He admitted in later life that he had only played truant once, 'and that was the vilest day of my life. When I came home my father had already been

Fritz Brahms in 1870.

Brahms told George Henschel that 'with his sister he had little in common; between his brother and himself there existed no intercourse whatever'.

The Great Fire of Hamburg in 1842.

informed of it, and I got a solid hiding'. But study did not absorb all his time. He had one abiding passion that was to provide relaxation late into his life: his tin soldiers. He had battalions of them which he continually arranged and rearranged; even in his revered old age he found pleasure in setting them out for the children of his friends.

Otherwise his childhood was mostly uneventful. He survived two disasters: the great fire of Hamburg in 1842 that swept through the tenements like tinder but avoided his area by a swift change of wind; and a road accident at the age of ten which incapacitated him for a few months, but otherwise left him unmarked.

Cossel allowed his pupil at the age of ten to appear in public, playing the piano part in a Beethoven quintet and a quartet by Mozart. As luck would have it, an American impresario who was talent-spotting in Europe, attended the boy's début. He saw the commercial possibilities and offered to make his fortune if he could be allowed to take him on a concert tour of America. Jakob Brahms was overwhelmed by the prospect of the vast sums offered and agreed on the spot. 'My father was a dear old man, very simple-minded and most unsophisticated', was Johannes' affectionate summing-up of his character in later years. So the Brahms family sold Christiane's small shop at a loss and prepared to embark for the promised land.

Cossel, however, was horrified. He knew that a series of catch-penny Wild West recitals would stunt the delicately forming genius of his pupil and he resisted with all his powers of persuasion. But in order to persuade parents struggling in poverty to give up such a seemingly heaven-sent opportunity, he would have to justify his faith in their son. To do this, he enlisted the aid of Eduard Marxsen – the finest teacher in Hamburg and his own former master – to take Johannes under his wing.

Marxsen needed some persuasion, but once he had heard the boy play he was so impressed that he decided to teach him without payment. Jakob Brahms was delighted with this turn of events and the dubious American tour was cancelled.

Johannes settled into a new and more rigorous routine. He was moved to another school, where he received a basic grounding in Latin and French and was drawn towards the literature of the German Romantics. He was also forced to take a more disciplined approach to the art of virtuosity under Marxsen, who first discouraged all attempts at composition and concentrated on keyboard technique. Gradually, however, he relented when he saw that Johannes had an urge towards composition that was as important as his desire to shine on the concert platform. The boy's first wayward attempts were given a structure based on a close study of Beethoven, Schubert, Mozart and, above all, Bach, who was little appreciated at the time. Thus at the very beginning of his career Brahms was drawn towards classical forms that would eventually help channel the flow of his deeply Romantic inclinations. Marxsen's influence was profound and Brahms's respect for his illustrious teacher never waned; for years after he had achieved the status of a master himself, he would still submit new works to him for criticism and advice.

All this was very gratifying to his parents, but it did nothing to pay the bills. To help the family economy, Brahms had to give badly paid lessons at the age of twelve, and when he was thirteen he began the drudgery that his father had escaped, playing dance music in the bars of the Gängviertel at night for a pittance, but as much ale as he could drink. Apart from the usual scenes of drunkenness and disorder that he witnessed, there was no shortage of prostitutes who made it their business to surround the boy as he churned out cheap music by the hour, using him to lure clients or making crude jokes to while away the time in between. In later years he referred to this period of his life with great distaste, once snapping to a friend who had raised women on too high a pedestal: 'That was my first impression of the love of women. And you expect me to honour them as you do!'

He found his escape in imagination. Instead of music, he placed a volume of poetry on the stand in front of him and read Eichendorff, Novalis, Heine or Hölderlin as he played. Their world of insatiable longings and transcendental nature-worship was a stark antidote to his own surroundings, but perhaps he was sustained by irony as much as by any escapist dream of forests,

12

Self-portrait of the author
E. T. A. Hoffman, who
exercised a great influence
over the young Brahms.

knights and fair maidens that the verses contained. He was, after all, surrounded by Lorelei.

Books were a continual source of intellectual nourishment to him. He began to collect old volumes from the bookstalls that stood on the bridges over the Hamburg canals and would copy down, in a series of notebooks, passages of verse or ideas that especially took his fancy. He called this personal anthology 'Young Kreisler's Treasury', styling himself on the ambiguous musician Kreisler, chief characters of Hoffmann's novel *Kater Murr* where an outrageous tomcat writes his autobiography on the back of Kreisler's musings on Art and Life. Brahms never lost his fascination with the grotesque and sinister world of Hoffmann's stories, or with the heightened sense of irony that they contain.

The hard work, the need to practise in piano shops or wherever he could steal a few minutes on a spare instrument, filled all his time. He often longed for the quiet morning hour when he could put his musical thoughts on paper, as he later told his friend, the poet Widmann: 'The best songs came into my head while brushing my boots before dawn.' Gradually, this all began to tell on him. He became nervous with fatigue and in the end, as he confessed, he could only walk along a street by grasping at trees to avoid falling down.

An opportunity for a holiday came from an unexpected quarter. Adolph Giessemann was an acquaintance of his father's from the Alster Pavilion. He owned a paper mill at Winsen, a village on the Rhine, and could sing and play the guitar. Hearing of young Brahms's gifts and sad plight, he offered to lodge him in the spring of 1847 so that he might give his thirteen-year-old daughter Leischen encouragement with her piano lessons.

Brahms never forgot the kindness of the Giessemann family. In later years he wrote:

I am indebted to the family for much love and friendship and my memory of [Adolph Giessemann] is of the most beautiful kind that the human heart can treasure.

Through them, he discovered nature. After the slums of Hamburg he was suddenly confronted with Eichendorff's forests, the Rhine of German legend, the light and air that invests Hölderlin's verse with its most poignant sense of loss. But there was also companionship, which he had lacked, for Leischen and he struck up an immediate friendship. She was exactly the kindred spirit he needed to share his enthusiasms, and they walked for miles through the countryside and read together in the evenings. Tieck's medieval romance *Magelone* was an especial favourite, and much later Brahms set the poems from it in his song-cycle *Die Schöne Magelone* as a tribute to the happiness of those days.

There was an opportunity to make music with the local community too. Brahms soon became friendly with Herr Blume, a bailiff who was also a good amateur musician, and they played

Canal in Hamburg. Brahms bought his first books from the stalls that stood nearby.

two-piano versions of Beethoven's works together. There was also a thriving male-voice choir who asked Brahms to direct and accompany them on the piano in the school or at the local inn where they met. He wrote two-part songs for them and particularly enjoyed the folk songs that formed the bulk of their repertoire. On a subsequent visit in the summer of 1848, he arranged two of these songs for them and his work with folk-song there influenced the composition of his first two piano sonatas at a slightly later date.

Brahms returned to Hamburg once a week for his lesson with Marxsen, and Leischen occasionally went with him. They travelled down the Rhine by steamer – a trip arranged by her uncle, who ran buffets on the new local railway and the Rhine steamboats. She would stay with the Brahms family overnight and her father sometimes paid for the pair of them to visit the Hamburg opera, where Brahms heard *The Marriage of Figaro* for the first time. Although they eventually drifted apart, as is often the case with the friends of early youth, Brahms was able to repay some of her parents' kindness by arranging a scholarship for Leischen's daughter in Vienna forty years afterwards.

Revolutionary fervour spread through Europe in 1848, but left Brahms untouched. He spent the summer in Winsen, and on returning to Hamburg in September he had more important worries than the mild democratic reforms that had transformed his home town's paternal government. He had left school, and must make his living in his chosen career of concert pianist. Although still playing at night in the Gängviertel bars and at the occasional private party, he also launched himself publicly at a concert in September. Here he bowed to the prevailing taste for flashy Lisztian pyrotechnics by including such pieces as Döhler's *William Tell* Fantasy, although a fugue by Bach showed where his real sympathies lay. A further concert in April 1849 was more ambitious: the obligatory bravura piece was Thalberg's *Don Juan Fantasy*, and he supplied his own *Fantasy on a Favourite Waltz*, which has not survived. However, the real musical meat was Beethoven's *Waldstein Sonata*.

Public and press were favourable, but cool. The emergence of a sixteen-year-old virtuoso with a markedly eccentric sense of programming could not really be expected to blaze the musical skies in the trail of Liszt's comet, and Brahms's own attitude did little to help, for he seems to have had no real liking for performance; composition was gradually taking complete hold of his mind. At this time it must have seemed a maelstrom of possibilities, although no youthful composition from this period survives the later bonfires he made of all his earliest works.

Apart from his serious attempts, congenial hack-work also came his way: he arranged popular pieces for bands and ensembles and even supplied slight salon pieces himself. These were all published under pseudonyms and some of doubtful authenticity have been unearthed this century.

By 1851 he had written his first extant work – the Scherzo in E flat minor, for piano, and his first two piano sonatas – in C major and F sharp minor – were begun the following year. He had also composed a number of songs including the fine *Liebestreu*. A friend, Louise Japha, persuaded him to leave some of his works at the hotel where Robert Schumann and his internationally famous pianist wife, Clara, were staying in Hamburg. But the Schumanns were too busy to look at them, and the parcel containing them was returned unopened. This disappointed the shy young composer,

Robert and Clara Schumann in Hamburg.

but the two celebrities were soon to atone a hundredfold for their neglect. Another distant encounter, with the virtuoso violinist Joseph Joachim, occurred when Brahms heard him play Beethoven's Violin Concerto in Hamburg. He could not possibly have realised the effect this man would also have on his life.

So Brahms continued playing in bars, giving lessons, writing hack pieces and arranging others, and must have seemed to lack all sense of direction to his parents, who could not perceive the inner fires that smouldered in their son. Only Marxsen did not waver in his faith, for he had sensed genius in this obscure boy from the back streets and knew that he was only marking time, awaiting his opportunity.

Often, when potent forces are gathered in readiness, something seemingly insignificant is needed to spark off an event, and nothing or nobody could have seemed less significant than the fantastic Eduard Reményi. Yet he was to be the dazzling catalyst of Brahms's new career.

2 Escape

Brahms first met Reményi at the house of a rich Hamburg merchant in 1851 when both were engaged the same evening to provide music for a party. Although he was only three years older than Brahms, Reményi was a worldly figure. This Jewish-Hungarian violinist had been actively involved in the 1848 revolutions, fleeing in 1849 from Budapest before the Habsburg military backlash. Like Wagner, who was also on the run for his part in the Dresden revolution, he was seeking refuge where he could, and Hamburg tolerated his kind for a while.

Brahms and Reményi in 1853. Reményi is seated so that the diminutive Brahms is not overshadowed.

It was not just his glamour as a revolutionary or his flashy virtuoso's personality that impressed the reserved young Brahms, but his fiery interpretations of 'gypsy' music, which was synonymous with Hungary in those days. Its wayward rhythms and distinct ethnic colour were a revelation that Brahms never forgot, and he was so entranced that he struck up a professional acquaintance, performing with the violinist at private functions for several months. The Hamburg police then decided that all Hungarian refugees posed a political threat, and expelled them. Reményi left in haste for America, but returned late the following year, contacted Brahms and suggested the two collaborate on a concert tour of north-east Germany. Brahms was delighted with the idea, and the two set off in the spring of 1853. For Brahms, it was to be a *Wanderjahr* that changed his life utterly.

At first they kept a low profile, beginning their tour at Winsen where Brahms's old friends gave them an enthusiastic welcome, ensuring that their concert was a sell-out. They stayed there almost a month, then moved on to Celle where Brahms was also known. Their recital in this town was remarkable chiefly for Brahms's transposition of Beethoven's C minor violin sonata into C sharp minor as he sat at a piano pitched a semitone too low. Brahms thought this quite normal, but Reményi was so impressed that he announced it to the audience, uncharacteristically allowing a little limelight to fall on his accompanist. He was not to be so easily pleased as the tour progressed.

In Lüneberg, which they visited next, Brahms's old duet partner, Herr Blume, threw a party in their honour and their concert was so successful that it had to be repeated the next day.

All this was very pleasant, but Reményi was after larger fish. He judged the time ripe to visit an old student friend – Joachim – who had risen to international fame and was now the leader of the King of Hanover's orchestra.

Brahms was overwhelmed with shyness when he met the great violinist he had admired from afar, but he was not at first called on to speak: Reményi did all that. He talked endlessly of his triumphs and expectations and reminisced about his student days with Joachim. When Joachim could silence Reményi's rapturous self-congratulation for a moment, however, he turned his attention to Brahms. Gradually he drew him out of his shell, and soon the young composer was seated at the piano playing his two sonatas and his Scherzo in E. Joachim was overwhelmed by the 'undreamt-of originality and power' of the music, as he later said, so that, despite their differing positions in the world, and their three-year age gap, there and then the two became mutual admirers and good friends.

Brahms wrote to his parents immediately telling them the great news, and his mother replied in rapture:

Your great hour has come. You must thank Divine Providence which has sent an angel to lead you out of the darkness into the world where there are human beings who appreciate your worth.

Hanover in the 1850s.

Joseph Joachim in 1853 – a pencil sketch by Laurens. Brahms was overwhelmed by shyness when he met the great violinist, who later befriended him.

But the Hanover idyll was brief. Joachim arranged a concert for them before the King, but the police discovered afterwards that Reményi was a notorious revolutionary. The two were ignominiously expelled from Hanover, though not before Joachim had given them a letter of introduction to Liszt's artistic haven in Weimar, written rapturously to Schumann about Brahms and pressed the young composer to stay with him when the inevitable break occurred with the vain and temperamental Reményi.

Brahms approached Weimar with trepidation. Although he had virtually retired from the concert platform, the forty-year-old Liszt was still the legendary master-pianist of his generation: a glittering company that included such supreme technicians as Moschelles, Thalberg and Pixis. As such, he was the Paganini of the piano, a man of whom Clara Schumann had written in 1831:

He can be compared with no other virtuoso . . . He causes fright and astonishment.

Yet this was not all. He reigned in splendour over an artistic court at the Villa Altenberg – home of his rich and unbalanced

The Residenz, Weimar.
Liszt kept artistic open
house at the Villa Altenberg
nearby.

mistress, the Princess Sayn-Wittgenstein – and as such led one of the factions that had split musical Germany apart.

The bitter controversies of these rival theories seem largely irrelevant to us now, propelled as they were by the characters and prejudices of their followers, but they had great influence on the shaping of Brahms's musical idiom and were largely responsible for his later painstaking and reticent approach to composition. On one side there were the classicists, who based themselves in Leipzig and followed the classical ideals of Mendelssohn (then dead for seven years) and on the other, the progressive 'New German' faction, broadly based on the theories of Berlioz, which tended towards a general loosening of form to express emotional states and literary ideas. Like all artistic theories, much depends on whether genius manipulates them or not. Liszt, and later Wagner, could produce tone-poems and operas that are masterpieces, but often the New Germans degenerated into undisciplined self-indulgence and virtuosity for its own sake. Brahms at this time inclined to neither school, although he would soon find himself temperamentally at odds with both. But at the Villa Altenberg he could judge the New Germans at their most dramatic and bizarre.

Here Liszt kept open house for all musicians sympathetic to his ideals, so Brahms and Reményi found themselves thrust into a glittering company of young artists and composers that included Tausig and Cornelius, and the popular and prolific Raff. That

Franz Liszt, the legendary master pianist of his generation.

Brahms felt out of his depth is certain. Although unprepossessing from the outside, the Villa Altenberg contained a treasure-house of antiques. As he wandered about its salons, the young slum-boy must have been struck dumb by such curios as Beethoven's Bechstein piano and death-mask. The intellectual revels regularly carried on until dawn, shocking the staid inhabitants of the provincial town and causing a scandal throughout Europe. All conversation was carried on in French, Liszt claiming he had forgotten his native tongue, and as Brahms's French was imperfect, he was even more alienated. The Princess herself was the final shock. His Lutheran propriety must have been jolted by her Catholic religiosity as she stalked about in a loose black gown, smoking cigars and haranguing her guests with sentimental banter and arty intensity. Ernest Newman later called her a 'half-cracked religious blue stocking', but to be fair to Liszt he was beginning to chafe at her bit, and he also received the young Brahms with kindness and courtesy.

Joachim, naturally, had painted him in the finest colours, and Liszt was so intrigued that he called the young composer to the piano to perform his compositions to the assembled *cognoscenti*. At this point Brahms completely lost his nerve and could not be induced to play a note. Liszt took his manuscripts from his hands and played the Scherzo in E flat at sight with such technical assurance that Brahms could only marvel and sink deeper into his chair.

Accounts do not agree on the events of the next few weeks, but there is no doubt that the longer he stayed in this continuous gathering of wealthy Bohemians, the less sympathy he felt for their cause. A breach with Reményi was also in the air. Brahms later wrote of him: 'I could never get Reményi to tell the truth, he was such an awful liar.' Although he did not dislike Liszt as a man and continued to admire his pianism, the cult of Liszt and, above all, his music – which seemed to paint picture postcards of emotion – grew more and more distasteful to him. The logical structures of Bach and Beethoven which were meat and drink to Brahms bore no comparison to the flashy effects relying on literary support that he discerned in the music he heard performed at Weimar. There was something of the intolerance of youth for anything that does not fit in with its chosen ideals in this approach, and it is true we would remove several primary colours from the musical spectrum by expunging Liszt, yet Brahms had stubbornly made up his mind.

Whether Brahms actually did fall asleep as Liszt played his own piano sonata, or whether this was just another of Reményi's 'lies', is not clear, but Brahms was already displaying the general lack of tact that became his hallmark in later years, and could not disguise his animosity to everything the Villa Altenberg stood for. Liszt noticed, but did not take deep offence. Reményi, however, was shocked. His companion's boorishness could ruin everything he

21

The Market Square, Göttingen. Brahms spent a happy month in this university town under Joachim's wing.

had so meticulously arranged. He immediately declared himself a slavish follower of Liszt, and dissociated himself utterly from Brahms.

Isolated and abandoned in an unknown town, Brahms poured out his distress to the only sympathetic friend he knew. He wrote to Joachim:

Reményi is leaving Weimar without me. It is *his* wish, for my manner could not have given him the slightest pretext for doing so.

Joachim replied, warmly inviting him to stay at Göttingen where he was attending lectures on philosophy and history, and Brahms set off at once.

He spent a heady month in the sleepy university town, enjoying the lifestyle of a German student without any of the attendant bookwork. Many years later he celebrated the impassioned debates and boisterous drinking sessions of this brief taste of university in his lighthearted *Academic Festival Overture*, but at the time he was working on a third piano sonata which shows something of the unavoidable influence of Liszt. Brahms discovered that he and Joachim were firm friends and he looked to the older and more famous musician for advice on composition. Joachim, who was then a moderately well-known composer, was pleased to give it, and so the weeks passed agreeably for both.

Meanwhile, his family were growing anxious. They could not understand why a recital tour that had begun so auspiciously should end so abruptly, and offered to scrape together all available

22

Stolzenfels on the Rhine, where Brahms passed a 'heavenly summer' in 1853.

funds to help him continue the tour. When he refused their offer, Frau Brahms wrote in despair:

How can you live away from home without money? If you have to get every little thing from Joachim, you will be under too great an obligation to the gentleman . . . You understand people too little and trust them too much.

So Joachim took up his pen, writing in his defence:

Your Johannes has stimulated my work as an artist to an extent beyond my hopes . . . His purity, his independence, young though he is, and the singular wealth of his heart and intellect find sympathetic utterance in his music, just as his whole nature will bring joy to all who come into spiritual contact with him. How splendid it will be when his artistic powers are revealed in a work accessible to all!

Such praise from a musician of Joachim's standing overjoyed Brahms's family who now began to realise that they had something more than a virtuoso in their son.

Brahms had glimpsed success, and knew he must take hold of it soon or it might slip from his grasp. He had been praised but not

23

published, and this now became his dearest wish. At last, he grew restless in Göttingen and decided to set off once more in search of musical contacts.

Joachim wanted him to visit Robert Schumann, whom he revered as a composer, immediately and, after receiving his letter, the Schumanns were anxious to meet him. But Brahms still remembered the manuscripts returned unopened and this snub, combined with an ignorance of Schumann's music, made him unenthusiastic. He decided to go on a walking tour down the Rhine in order to take stock of his position. Joachim organised a concert which provided Brahms with the necessary funds, and with Joachim's letter of introduction in his rucksack he set off.

He was once more enchanted by the legendary Rhine and spent five weeks progressing from town to town. He wrote to his friend Blume:

I have passed a heavenly summer . . . After spending some gloriously inspiring weeks with Joachim . . . I have been rambling about . . . to my heart's desire, on the sacred Rhine.

Thanks to Joachim, he had made useful contacts: the conductor Wasielewski in Bonn, who also encouraged him to visit Schumann, the Diechmanns in Mehlem – Schumann enthusiasts too, whose collection of the composer's works Brahms discovered with delight – Carl Reinicke and Ferdinand Hiller in Cologne, both influential conductors. And it was in Cologne in September that Brahms finally summoned up his courage, took a train to Düsseldorf and went straight to Robert Schumann's home.

He found the great Romantic in bourgeois circumstances, which were much more to Brahms's taste. Robert, Clara and their six children lived in a modest but comfortable house, with no intellectual coteries or disciples waiting to intimidate the young man. They welcomed him enthusiastically and Brahms in turn warmed to their unaffected goodwill. Soon he was playing his Sonata in C to Schumann, and Clara was immediately summoned into the room with the call: 'You will hear music unlike any you have heard before.' They sat, transfigured, as he played. Later, Schumann wrote:

He began to uncover truly marvellous regions . . . there were sonatas more like symphonies in disguise.

And Clara confided to her diary:

The music he played was so masterly that it seems God sent him into the world complete.

The Schumanns insisted that he stay in Düsseldorf as long as possible, and arranged lodgings nearby so that he could visit them daily. Their diaries are full of enthusiastic references to him, a

Düsseldorf, where Brahms was acclaimed by the Schumanns.

favourite description being 'young eagle', and in a letter to Joachim, Schumann described him as 'the one who is to come'.

Brahms met many of the Schumann circle during his stay. One, the twenty-four-year-old Albert Dietrich, a pupil of Schumann's, has left an invaluable account of the the friendship that grew up between them. On meeting him he wrote:

The youthful, almost boyish-looking musician, with his high-pitched voice and long fair hair made a most attractive impression on me. I was particularly struck by the characteristic energy of the mouth and the serious depths in his blue eyes.

He also found his old friend Louise Japha, who had moved to Düsseldorf with her sister, and his intellectual horizons were broadened by mixing with as pleasant a group of artists and writers as it was possible to find. He was particularly taken with Bettina von Arnim, an artist whose husband Achim had published the *Knaben Wunderhorn* collection of German folk-songs and whose influence on the Romantic movement was seminal. During his stay, Brahms often appeared as soloist at these civilised gatherings of like-minded people and Dietrich has left us a description of one such recital:

He executed Bach's Toccata in F major and his own Scherzo with wonderful power and mastery, bending his head over the keys, and, as was his wont, in his excitement, humming the melody aloud as he played. He modestly deprecated the torrent of praise with which his performance was greeted. Everyone marvelled at his remarkable talent.

25

Brahms aged twenty. The pencil sketch by Laurens echoes Albert Dietrich's description of Brahms as a 'youthful, almost boyish-looking musician'.

Writing later to Ernst Naumann, Dietrich also gave his opinion of Brahms as a composer:

Brahms's compositions, written already in early youth, soar to great heights. If his music does recall anything it is the later Beethoven. Then there is a tinge of the folk song all through his works and this it is I believe which lends such a special fascination to all his music.

The folk-song element was one that Brahms openly acknowledged, telling Dietrich that he often attracted musical themes by thinking of folk-song words.

Brahms's exuberant sense of fun found full vent during his stay. Dietrich records: 'With the boisterousness of youth he would run up the stairs, knock at my door with both fists, and, without awaiting a reply, burst into the room.'

He was 'blunt and full of wild freaks'. On an outing to nearby Grafenberg, he pulled turnips up from a field, 'cleaning them carefully, he playfully offered them to the ladies as refreshment.'

In this atmosphere of general mirth, Schumann suggested a musical party game. Joachim was due later that month to give a concert, why not compose a composite violin sonata for him as a welcoming gift? So it was agreed: Dietrich wrote the first movement, Brahms a scherzo and Schumann an intermezzo and finale. They adopted Joachim's personal motto FAE, standing for *Frei Aber Einsam* (Free But Lonely), as a theme unifying each movement and kept their authorship anonymous as a further conundrum. Joachim duly arrived, played the sonata and guessed the composers of each movement without any trouble at all. Brahms's scherzo is still in the repertoire, the only portion of the sonata to be played at all regularly. The dotted rhythm that gives it its powerful momentum is worthy of the mature composer: from the very beginning of his career, the unmistakable 'Brahms' sound had emerged. From then on Brahms too adopted a personal motto, based on Joachim's but with a significant change. His became the defiant *Frei Aber Froh* (Free But Happy), and appears many times in works with a particular emotional significance after that date.

Before Brahms left Düsseldorf, Schumann decided to help him as much as he could. He wrote to his Leipzig publishers, Breitkopf and Härtel, suggesting they consider anything the young man had to offer. Brahms was delighted when he heard of this and began a thorough revision of his compositions to date. He then left the Schumanns, rejoining Joachim in Hanover, and it was there that, opening the *Neue Zeitschrift für Musik* on 28 October, he had the greatest shock of all.

Schumann, who had founded the paper to combat 'Philistines' in the year Brahms was born, had eventually retired from its staff and had not contributed anything to its pages for over ten years. Now he had sent them an article entitled 'New Ways' which was nothing more than a high-flown hymn of praise to Brahms:

26

The first letter Brahms
wrote to his publishers,
Breitkopf and Härtel, 1853.

I felt certain one man would appear fated to express the spirit of the times in the loftiest and most ideal manner, who would gain mastery, not by degrees, but immediately, springing like Minerva fully armed from the head of Jove. And now he is here, a young man at whose cradle graces and heroes stood guard. He is called Johannes Brahms . . . When he holds his magic wand over the massed resources of chorus and orchestra, we shall be granted marvellous insights into spiritual secrets.

Brahms was elated, but also apprehensive. He was only twenty years old, immature for his age, unknown, and yet had been singled out as a child of destiny by one of Germany's leading composers. Great things would be expected of him, animosities would be aroused. He wrote to Schumann from Hanover on 16 November:

The public praise that you have deigned to bestow upon me will have so greatly increased the expectations of the musical world regarding my work that I do not know how I shall manage to do even approximate justice to it. Above all, it will compel me to exercise the greatest caution in my choice of pieces for publication. I am thinking that I shall not publish any of my trios, but shall select the sonatas in C and F sharp minor to be my opus 1 and 2. Opus 3 will be the songs and opus 4 will be the Scherzo in E flat minor. You will readily understand that I am straining every nerve to bring as little disgrace as possible on your name.

27

Leipzig, centre of the
Classicist school.

None of the trios he mentions has survived, with the possible
exception of one in A major which was discovered and published
in 1938. It had no title-page, but strongly suggests the wayward
and explosive romanticism of the young Brahms. It is not a great
work, but is an interesting musical curiosity. He also destroyed a
string quartet before submitting the works he intended to show to
the publishers to a rigorous revision.

Arriving in Leipzig at the end of November, Brahms found
Breitkopf and Härtel willing to print his works. An ardent
Schumannite, Heinrich von Sahr, invited Brahms to stay and at
once proceeded to introduce him to the musical doyens of the city,
including the conductor Julius Rietz; the pianist and composer of
bravura concertos, Ignaz Moscheles, who had known Beethoven,
and the influential leader of the Leipzig Gewandhaus orchestra,
Ferdinand David. He also met a young music student, Otto
Grimm, with whom he found much in common.

After rejecting the New German camp at the Villa Altenberg,
Brahms now had to decide whether the Leipzig classicists were
more to his taste. Leipzig, too, looked askance at Schumann's
'young eagle' for it was not the first time Schumann had hailed as a
genius someone who later became a mediocrity. Naturally, many
thought that Brahms was yet another of Schumann's nine-day
wonders.

But Brahms was ready for them. With David, he performed a
violin sonata he had recently written and was well received at

various salons before giving a series of public concerts. He then played his First Piano Sonata at the Gewandhaus on 17 December. The great Berlioz was present and was so impressed that he publicly embraced Brahms in the foyer. Reviews were mixed, however. Although the musical journal *Signale* called Brahms: 'An artist by God's gift . . . he will . . . someday be what Schumann has prophesied', another paper announced that he 'would never be a star of the first magnitude'.

Brahms was untroubled by this, for audiences were largely favourable. Liszt had also attended his Gewandhaus concert. He did not hold the Altenberg episode against him and when the young composer visited him at his hotel, he received him kindly, later writing to the pianist Hans von Bülow that he was 'genuinely interested' in Brahms.

Sahr put him in touch with another publishing house, Senff. They accepted six songs as Op.6, although they put his violin sonata on one side as they did not deal in music for that instrument. This sonata was eventually lost, although Dietrich was shown the violin part nineteen years later and 'deeply regretted that the piano part of it could not be found'. Brahms gave them his newest piano sonata, in F minor, Op.5, as a substitute. This striking work is on an epic scale, the romantic Brahms filling the score with funeral marches and echoes of drum beats, loosely taking a rapturous poem by Sternau as a programme: 'The twilight draws in, and two heavens are held in a blessed embrace as the moon shines down.' Brahms would never again wear his heart on his sleeve as thoroughly as he did in this sonata.

Leaving Leipzig with a feeling that its musical faction was too ossified for his needs, Brahms returned to Hamburg in time to spend Christmas with his awed and adoring family. Before the year was out, he had received his first published works and immediately sent them off to Schumann with this letter:

Herewith, I take the liberty of sending you your first foster-children . . . in their new garb they seem to me too prim and embarrassed – almost philistine. I still cannot accustom myself to seeing these guileless children of nature in their smart new clothes.

The family spent that Christmas and New Year in a heady whirl of celebration. His father had been appointed to the Hamburg Theatre orchestra, and now the seasonal goose and Frau Brahms's special egg-nog were flavoured with the unfamiliar taste of success. In nine months the young Johannes had achieved unbelievable fame, and now he let his native city know he was a force that could not be ignored. He toured the Gängviertel bars, loudly banging out the vulgar tunes he had been forced to play there for a pittance: a final gesture of defiance aimed at the squalor that so nearly absorbed his genius forever.

Yet even as Brahms basked in the triumphs of that year, tragedy was gathering in the wings.

3 Storm and Stress

Only those closest to him knew that Schumann was treading a mental tightrope. Brahms had noticed a slight 'nervous disorder' the previous year, but did not realise the extent of its hold. A battle with insanity had raged within him for years: the wayward rhythms in his later music and the characters of Florestan and Eusebius in his critical writings could not exorcise the problem. Gradually, stresses of work, his conducting career (which he would not give up despite his obvious inability to cope with its technical, diplomatic and administrative demands), aggravated the condition. He fell into deeper and longer periods of reverie, grew more involved with the new Spiritualist Church and was convinced that the dead were speaking to him from the 'Other Side'.

Brahms had taken lodgings in Hanover in January 1854, and was spending a carefree time in the company of Joachim and Grimm. He had composed the bulk of his Piano Trio in B, Op.8, and had grown friendly with the pianist Hans von Bülow, a Wagnerian who nevertheless was the first artist to play one of Brahms's works in public. When the Schumanns arrived at the end of the month, Brahms was overjoyed. These were, he said, 'high festival days that make you really live'. At a concert arranged in his honour Schumann heard his Fourth Symphony, and Joachim played a work specially written for him: the Fantaisie for Violin and Orchestra. Clara performed Beethoven's *Emperor* Concerto, and Schumann's beautiful and extraordinary oratorio *Paradise and the Peri* ended the programme. It concerned the longings of a demi-spirit for the gates of a Christian heaven, and although an early work it seems appropriate to his preoccupations at this time.

After a great deal of music and a great deal of eating and drinking, the Schumanns returned to Düsseldorf in February. Here the darkness his young friends had dispelled for a while closed in more dangerously than before. He wrote to Joachim:

It is a week since we sent you and your friends a sign, but I have often written to you spiritually, and will later reveal the invisible writing behind this letter . . . It is growing darker.

He began to hear voices again; angels and demons echoed through his divided nature. The spirits of Mendelssohn and Schubert dictated a theme which was none other than that of his own Violin Concerto, and commanded him to write variations on it. As he worked at the music on the night of 27 February he could suddenly bear it no longer. Dressed only in a robe and slippers, he ran out of his house and threw himself into the Rhine. A barge rescued him, but could not salvage his mind. He was now totally insane.

Joachim read of his friend's attempted suicide in the *Cologne Gazette*. He wrote to Dietrich in Düsseldorf:

If you bear the least friendship for Brahms and me, relieve us from our misery and write immediately whether Schumann's state is really as serious as the papers say and give us news of every change in his condition.

Brahms was the only friend without commitments, and when Dietrich's reply confirmed the reports he left for Düsseldorf on 3 March. There he found his friend and mentor begging for treatment. The following day Schumann entered a private asylum at Endenich, near Bonn, as a voluntary patient.

Clara was on the verge of despair. Her beloved husband, whom she had defied her father to marry and who had been her strength and comfort for over fourteen years, was too ill to see her; she was expecting her seventh child and had no financial support whatsoever. Only the arrival of Brahms, followed closely by Grimm and Joachim, kept her sane herself.

Dietrich continued to send reports to Schumann's friends. On 19 March he wrote to Naumann:

There is no doubt that the seeds of Schumann's illness have long lain dormant in him. His constant cerebral activity . . . his almost complete severance from the outer world, his leaning towards spiritualism . . . all this has combined to unbalance this great and noble mind, and perhaps darken it forever.

Only Brahms could stay for any length of time, and he was delighted to do so. He taught Clara's pupils when she was unwell, ran errands, acted as surrogate father to the Schumann children, and played to her both Schumann's music and his own latest compositions, including the newly completed piano trio. As she listened to this passionate music, her reserved heart softened to the young man who was so different from her husband. Dietrich wrote:

Brahms has written a beautiful trio . . . he is a man whom one ought to take as an example in every respect; with all his depths, natural, fresh and cheerful, and quite untouched by modern unhealthy tendencies.

and Clara confided to her diary:

Brahms does not say much, but his expression shows how much he grieves with me for the loved one he regards so highly . . . From such a young man, I am doubly aware of the sacrifice, for sacrifice it surely is for anyone to be with me at this time.

31

A page from the manuscript
of Brahms's Schumann
Variations, Op.9. Schumann
called them 'magnificent'.

Following the birth of her child, whom she named Felix after
Mendelssohn, she wrote to Brahms, who was still looking after her
home: 'When I look at the darling baby at my side and think of his
dear father who, far removed from everything that he loves . . .
does not even know of this child's existence, I feel as though my
heart must break with grief and pain.' Returning to her house, she
immediately made plans to move to more economical quarters.
Brahms helped her move and took great care of Schumann's
papers. Writing to Dietrich, he says: 'I have, to my great joy,
arranged Schumann's library of books and music and now sit there
the whole day long and study.'

There was more cheerful news of Schumann's condition at this
time. Clara, after recuperating in Ostend, felt strong enough in
August to resume her concert tours. She left Brahms in
Düsseldorf, though she took some of his music with her, and
began her long series of recitals in which she made the Brahms
cause her own.

Although Brahms had remained outwardly cheerful for Clara's
sake, the events of the previous few months cut deep into his
heart. But his compositions show little of the emotional turmoil he
was undergoing: he produced two sets of variations on themes by

Schumann, one as a gift for Clara when she returned with her new baby and the other on the 'spirit' theme; a set of variations on a Hungarian theme also amused him, and he finished the Four Ballades, Op.10. The first, based on the grim Scottish ballad *Edward* which Julius Allgeyer had introduced to him in Düsseldorf, bows to the German Romantic obsession with Scotland but is otherwise directly inspired by Chopin's set. All these show poignancy, but little of the real musical matter of his mind, which was nothing less than an abortive attempt at a symphony where he struggled unsuccessfully to come to terms with Schumann's confinement and what he realised was a growing emotional dependence on Clara.

Now, in her absence, his emotions came to a head. Leaving the Schumann household in the capable hands of their governess, he set off for a walking tour of the Black Forest to calm himself. It was useless. Writing to Herr Blume he said:

The Black Forest, where Brahms went to think through his relationship with Clara. He wrote to her, 'Not once on my whole journey have I been lighthearted and cheerful . . . All about me there is the darkness of midnight.'

I had no idea how much I was attached to the Schumanns, how I lived in them; everything seemed barren and empty, every day I wanted to go back and had to travel by railway to move forward quickly and forget turning back. It was no good; I have reached Ulm, on foot and by rail; I am going to return quickly and would prefer to await Frau Schumann in Düsseldorf than wander around in darkness.

And to Clara from the waiting room on Ulm station:

I cannot stand it any longer; I am coming back today . . . I should not have enjoyed a single moment of the trip. The names Tübingen, Lichtenstein, Schaffhausen which otherwise would have thrilled me with joy, leave me cold, so dull and colourless does everything seem to me.

It is not surprising that Brahms should have responded to Clara in this fashion. She was a beautiful and cultured woman, only thirty-five years old, and had shown Brahms more kindness and understanding than any woman apart from his mother. He was truly on the horns of a dilemma, for Schumann showed signs of recovery and in his lucid intervals wrote admiringly to Brahms:

If only I could come to you myself and see you again and hear your magnificent Variations . . . how one recognises you in the richest brilliance of your imagination and again in your profound artistry in a way that I have not yet learned to know.

Brahms wrote back humbly:

The all too generous praise which you . . . bestow on my Variations has filled me with hope and joy. Ever since the spring I have been diligently studying your works.

He visited the afflicted composer when he could and played the piano for him, but the recovery was only to be temporary. A slow dissolution of the brain cells linked to possible tertiary syphilis was eventually diagnosed, and it soon became clear that Schumann could only get worse.

Brahms wrote to Clara declaring his love on 15 December:

Would to God that I were allowed this day instead of writing this letter to you to repeat to you with my own lips that I am dying of love for you. Tears prevent me from saying more . . .

Then, learning that Clara was giving a recital in Hamburg a few days later, he rushed there on the earliest train and insisted on introducing her to his parents. They got on well, and Clara noted how much she felt at home with these 'simple, though respectable people'. But if his family thought Brahms was going to spend Christmas with them, they were wrong. He hurried back to Düsseldorf with Clara, and was absent from Hamburg at Christmas for the first time in his life.

This was all very puzzling to his parents and they were uneasy. Marxsen, however, was exasperated. Brahms had spent a year living in virtual retirement from a world that had been aroused with expectations of a *Wunderkind*, and it cut no ice with him that the prodigy preferred to exchange counterpoint exercises with Joachim than go out and amaze the world. Brahms, however, was immovable. He remained in Düsseldorf, teaching, admiring Clara from a distance, and watching over Schumann's deteriorating health. After visiting him in February 1855, Brahms wrote to Clara that he had played duets with him, then taken him out for a walk:

It was very fine to see the heavy doors, which are usually bolted, opened for us . . . He was very pleased with my Hungarian hat just as he used to be in the old days . . . So we went to the cathedral, and to the Beethoven monument, after which I brought him back to the road . . .

And yet he was still torn between them: 'You have no idea how indispensable your presence is to me, you have not the remotest conception', he wrote to Clara that same month.

At last Clara shook him out of his torpor and persuaded him to join Joachim and herself on a concert tour in November. They visited Danzig, and the concert was such a success that Brahms continued on his own, playing Beethoven and Mozart concertos in Leipzig, Hamburg and Bremen, appearing as soloist with an orchestra for the first time. He was received with reserve, the thin-lipped Rubinstein remarking when he saw him play: 'For the salon he is not sufficiently at ease, for the concert room, not fiery enough; for the country, not primitive enough; for the city, not cosmopolitan enough. I have but little faith in such natures.'

He was soon back in Düsseldorf. There he underwent another crisis, for all composition virtually ceased. He began living a restless, surface existence, moving about in a state of indecision for several months, giving concerts, staying in Hanover, revisiting Liszt briefly. The only constant was Clara, although he seemed to realise that his love might be hopeless, writing in December:

I regret every word I write to you which does not speak of love. You have taught me and are every day teaching me ever more to recognise and to marvel at what love, attachment and self-denial are . . . I wish I could always write to you from my heart, to tell you how deeply I love you, and can only beg you to believe it without further proof.

Clara later destroyed her letters to Brahms from this period, but she must have been attracted to this sturdy, good-looking genius who had been so full of pranks and animal exuberance on his first visit to the Schumann household. Yet she knew the dangers of gossip. Brahms's mention of self-denial is significant, for she clearly did not encourage his infatuation beyond the bounds of propriety.

On his twenty-third birthday the following May he was still in Düsseldorf. Here he received an anxious letter from his mother:

Tonight we were all rather jolly, we drank the health of all of you, especially of the poor sick man. Johannes, dear, if we only had the power to do something for the good of Schumann! I beg you not to take it too much to heart; you cannot help him, and it only does you harm.

Bonn: Brahms would take Schumann from his asylum at nearby Endenich and walk through the streets with him, 'to the cathedral, and to the Beethoven monument'.

Yet Brahms could not tear himself away. In a letter written to Clara at the end of the month we can see the full gaze of the lover on his beloved:

I should like to spend the whole day calling you endearing names and paying you compliments without ever being satisfied. If things go on much longer as they are at present I shall have some time to put you under glass or to have you set in gold.

Things, were not, however, destined to go on as they were for much longer. News of Schumann's condition became grave that spring. Brahms moved to Bonn to be close to him. Here he met Dietrich again and was introduced to Julius Stockhausen, the famous baritone. The meeting was important for Brahms and the two soon became firm friends, appearing together in Bonn and Cologne, where Stockhausen sang Brahms's songs with that mastery that soon made him their finest interpreter.

Brahms visited Schumann on his birthday, taking a large atlas with him: 'For a very long time he had been asking for a very large atlas', he told Clara; but when he gave it to him, he seemed oblivious of everything else, immediately settling down to make lists of names from its pages.

'I am living through dreadful days,' Clara wrote to Dietrich

from London. 'I played at the Philharmonic concert yesterday with a bleeding heart. I had had a letter from Johannes in the morning, which made me feel the utter hopelessness of my beloved husband's state, although he most lovingly tried to represent everything as mildly as possible.'

On her return on 4 July Brahms met Clara at Antwerp, and they went to Ostend together so that Brahms could see the sea for the first time. Returning together to Düsseldorf on 6 July, they awaited the inevitable tragic news. It came at the end of the month: Robert Schumann was dying.

Hurrying to Endenich, Clara was allowed to see her husband at last. Brahms reported the moving scene in a letter to Grimm:

He lay first for some time with closed eyes, and she knelt before him with greater calmness than one would think possible. But later on, he recognised her, and he did so again next day. Once he clearly wished to embrace her and flung his arms round her. Of course, he was past being able to talk any more, one could only make out single words, perhaps in imagination. But even that was bound to make her happy.

He died on 29 July 1856, and the funeral took place two days later. Only a few close friends were present, Brahms, with

Brahms at the piano, 1856.

Dietrich and Joachim, escorting the coffin. Clara wrote in her diary that night:

His dearest friends went in front, and I came (unnoticed) behind, and it was best that way . . . And so, with his going, all my happiness is ended. A new life now begins for me.

Soon, she must decide what part Brahms must play in that new life. They decided to go to Switzerland for a rest, accompanied by two of the Schumann children and by Brahms's sister Elise. Having suffered for years with headaches and having been a prisoner in Hamburg all her life, she was in sore need of a change as well: 'How glad I shall be if Elise benefits from this summer', Clara wrote to Frau Brahms. 'You know how heavy my heart is. I don't want to talk of it, my heart bleeds at once. Johannes is my true friend and protector – what a blessing that I have him!'

We know that Elise enjoyed her trip down the Rhine to Heidelberg and then on to Lakes Constance and Lucerne, but nothing at all is known of how Clara and Brahms felt. This journey was the touchstone of their emotions and perhaps, to adapt George Herbert, 'Love bade them welcome, but their souls drew back', for nothing came of it. The reasons are complex. To an idealistic young man like Brahms, romantic love would be one thing, but marriage quite another. An inveterate reader of medieval romance, his yearning for Clara was that of the knight for the unattainable lady, a courtly love for a perfect being entirely above him in every respect. He had been her champion through her long ordeal, but the ordeal was over and he was faced with the prospect of marrying a woman fourteen years his senior, of becoming step-father and part-provider to her seven children, and the romantic dream must have faded into the cold light of reality very suddenly indeed. Clara must also have known how unsuitable such a match would have been, for it was one thing to maintain a highly charged sentimental friendship but quite another to think of setting up home with someone so young and inexperienced. Self-denial was also a keynote. She felt the propriety of grief that afflicted so many nineteenth-century widows, a sense of the irreplaceable one great love whom it was only fitting to honour in mourning for the rest of her life. Both had their reasons, and each drew back from the ultimate test of their feelings, declaring that they would remain the closest of friends for the rest of their lives, which of course they did.

Even so, Brahms was shattered. Never would he open his heart to another woman in quite the same way as he had done to Clara. The Schumanns had burned him out between them and all passion was temporarily spent. From now on he would grow more introspective, less boisterous, more reserved. But immediately he needed a period of total change to heal his exhausted nerves. He took a conscious decision to leave high-strung Romanticism behind and to take refuge in a rational eighteenth-century world.

4 Recuperation

The principality of Lippe-Detmold, situated near Hanover, was an anachronism even in Germany's outmoded political structure. Its ruling prince and his sister, the Princess Fredericke, presided over a court where protocol was rigid and outward display essential. As such, it was one of the last survivors of an eighteenth-century style that Bismarck would soon make doubly irrelevant.

Fraulein von Meysenbug, a pupil of Clara Schumann's whom Brahms had taught briefly, had connections with the court and had arranged for Brahms to visit the prince as early as 1855. He had found a quiet backwater with an ancient, ivy-covered castle and classical *Residenz* set in stunning natural beauty, and had immediately warmed to the place. After spending several disorientated months early in 1857, sometimes in Hamburg, sometimes staying with Clara, giving concerts, toying with the idea of settling in Hanover or Düsseldorf or even Hamburg, he received an invitation to take up an official post in Detmold. He regarded this new offer as a godsend, and accepted.

His duties were not too heavy. He only had to spend three months at the end of each year at the court, where he gave lessons to the princess – a willing pupil who grew genuinely fond of him – conducted the choral concerts whose chorus included the prince himself, appeared as soloist with the court's fine orchestra, as well as playing in the prince's private chamber ensembles. His generous salary was supplemented by lessons given to court ladies, and he had adequate leisure time to compose and walk in the massive Teutoberger Forest nearby.

Brahms's love of forests was almost pagan and he drew something close to mystical strength from trees throughout his life. Florence May, who met the composer in 1871 at Lichtenthal, was struck by his early-morning walks in the woods nearby and records that, when she asked him how she could improve her piano technique quickly, he replied, 'You must walk continually in the forest' – 'and he meant what he said to be taken literally', she adds.

Soothed by the landscape into an Olympian calm, Brahms soon gained control of himself. Clara had moved to Berlin to take up a teaching post, and Brahms wrote to her there on 11 October:

Passions are not natural to mankind; they are always exceptions or excrescences. The ideal, genuine man is calm both in his joy and in his sorrow. The man in whom they overstep the limits should regard himself

40

as an invalid and seek a medicine for his life and for his health. Passions must quickly pass or they must be hunted out . . .

This is a new Brahms, harder, already more stoical, closer to the spirit of an emergent Germany that would find its public stance in Bismarck's phrase 'Blood and Iron'. But despite his new strength of will and the healing proximity of nature, he began to find Detmold claustrophobic. He was especially burdened by the prince's indifferent music, recording wryly to Clara in the same letter: 'I had to accompany the prince in his songs. I hope it won't happen often.'

He also found a lack of kindred spirits, although he struck up a close friendship with Carl von Meysenbug and enjoyed the company of Carl Bargheer, leader of the court orchestra: 'Bargheer is, as you may imagine, most pleasant to me here. Otherwise there is a complete lack of musical friends, except for a few ladies', he wrote to Joachim in December.

As he lacked social grace, he was often carelessly dressed and found himself constantly at odds with court rituals. The chocolate-box principality soon became oppressive, the toytown army must have diminished in his eyes to a replica of his own battalions of tin soldiers, and the continual bowing and scraping irked him sorely. He records one telling incident in a letter home:

The other day, I conducted my choral society, which is richly adorned with Serene Highnesses, without a necktie! Luckily I didn't have to feel embarrassed or vexed, as I only noticed it when I was going to bed!

The fact that he considered so trivial an omission worthy of embarrassment in the first place says much for the preoccupations of this court.

But for all his petty vexations he was composing steadily again. During his first visit to Detmold he wrote a nonet-serenade. It was his tribute to the 'entertainment' music of Haydn and Mozart, which he was often called upon to play at court concerts. He later expanded the score into his orchestral Serenade No. 1 in D, Op.11, where the flavour of autumnal walks in the Teutoberger Forest and the formal classicism of an eighteenth-century world are captured perfectly, pointing to the serenity of much music to come. It was Brahms's first successful attempt at writing purely for orchestral forces, although he was also engaged on a piano concerto which had grown out of a two-piano version of part of his rejected 'Schumann' symphony. This had eventually foundered at the climax of his involvement with the Schumanns when he had first felt that terror of comparison with Beethoven that was to shadow him all his life. Beethoven's symphonies were the supreme pinnacle of achievement to Brahms and he avoided the form for as long as possible. Yet he was feeling his way. The orchestral score of the Serenade was originally called 'Symphony-Serenade', before Brahms once more had doubts and crossed it out.

The Brandenburg Gate, Berlin.

His first term at Detmold ended in January 1858 and he would not have to return there until the following autumn. Relieved, he hurried back to Hamburg on the earliest stage-coach. Here, he seemed to lose any firm sense of direction, wandering from friend to friend and putting in the occasional appearance at the Hamburg *Singverein*. By February he had grown restless, writing to Clara:

I am never, or very seldom in the least bit pleased with myself. I never feel quite happy, but fluctuate between contentment and depression.

To snap himself out of these moods, he paid a fleeting visit to Berlin – then the most intellectually stimulating city in North Germany, capital of the expanding Prussian state – and enjoyed visiting art galleries and making the acquaintance of the art historian Hermann Grimm, eldest son of the collector of German folk-tales. He also saw Clara. On his return to Hamburg he heard from Joachim, who was then on a concert tour of England, inviting him to stay at Göttingen that summer when he returned. But Brahms was too impatient. He set off immediately and stayed with Otto Grimm until Joachim arrived, followed closely by Clara.

If Brahms was drawn back to the town by memories of his surrogate student days, he soon found cause for renewed delight in the university, for he met the daughter of a university professor, Agathe von Siebold, a girl of his own age. Once more, Brahms's

42

Agathe von Siebold, to whom Brahms became secretly engaged.

susceptible heart was touched and the two grew close. They seemed ideally suited in many ways: both grew ecstatic in the presence of nature and they enjoyed many long walks in the countryside nearby; both were intelligent and well read, and both were deeply musical. Brahms composed three new sets of songs for her during that summer and she sang them in a voice that Joachim compared to an Amati violin.

Clara caught the drift of events and, although Brahms attempted some clumsy diplomacy, she saw him put his arm round the girl and left Göttingen petulantly. Nothing could be done about that and Brahms stayed on, growing more deeply attached to Agathe. He refused the offer of a post in Cologne because it would have taken up all his time, and was reluctant to return to Detmold when his duties called him back in October.

On his second visit he found the tin-pot principality more irritating than ever, though he warmed once more to an autumn spent among its fields and forests. His love for Agathe seemed to make him utterly light-headed as he wrote: 'I was in ecstasies. I thought of music alone . . . If things go on in this way, I will probably evaporate as a musical chord and float away into the atmosphere.' He composed his *Ave Maria*, Op.12 for women's voices, more songs for Agathe and the *Funeral Hymn*, Op.13 – first of many dark meditations on death. Half-way through his term he wrote home: 'Thank goodness my time is half over, the princess has told me so with sighs. She is the only person I care for, except Bargheer.'

In January 1859 he was liberated and hurried back to Göttingen to try out his songs with Agathe. He also carried the completed score of his new piano concerto, which was scheduled for its first performance in Hanover, under Joachim, on the twenty-second of the month. But the romance was the talk of Göttingen. Only Brahms seemed unaware that he was expected to announce an engagement. For him, love alone was everything and he had already exchanged rings with Agathe in a secret ceremony. After a fortnight he left for Hanover to supervise the last rehearsal of his new work, and it was there that he received a letter from Otto Grimm reminding him that it would be more tactful to make his intentions regarding Agathe public for the sake of propriety. Brahms was distressed by the letter, but was too concerned with the concert to reply immediately.

At its première, the Piano Concerto in D minor, Op.15, was received with polite, if slightly uncomprehending interest, but when it was performed at Leipzig five days later under Julius Rietz it was a complete disaster. Brahms wrote to Clara:

At the rehearsals it met with total silence and at the performance (where hardly three people raised their hands to clap) it was regularly hissed. But all this made no impression on me. I quite enjoyed the other music.

Behind his mask of laconic unconcern Brahms was bitterly

disappointed, especially as a bad press followed in the wake of the Leipzig performance. The *Leipziger Signalen* saw through to its symphonic origins and called it: 'A symphony with obbligato piano part. The solo area is thoroughly unpleasant and the orchestral writing is a series of slashing chords.' The *Neue Zeitschrift für Musik* also commented on a 'lack of outer effect', but added: 'The poetic material of the concerto is a true mark of important original creativity.'

Brahms sent these cuttings together with others of a generally disapproving nature to Clara, who replied: 'Such vile rubbish, so low . . . only deserves contempt.'

Yet it is not surprising that the concerto mystified audiences used to Liszt and Chopin. In their display concertos the orchestra was merely a camp-follower and the piano a dazzling centrepiece for virtuoso fingers. Brahms's concerto combined high dramatic tension with symphonic thought and the piano and orchestra were intellectual equals, pursuing the musical argument together, which was entirely out of keeping with the times. Brahms, too, must have seen the work in a new light. It was a summing-up of old passions evoked largely by the Schumann period; the music had worked them out of his system and when they were presented objectively in the concert hall he may not have known how to take them any more than his audience did.

Whatever his feelings about the music, the reception definitely made him distrust emotions and made him more firmly resolved not to tie himself down. As with Clara, he drew back from Agathe, terrified of that final commitment to domesticity. His response to Grimm's letter was to write an impulsive and tactless *cri de coeur* to the girl: 'I love you. I must see you again. But I can't be tied down. Write to me to tell me if I can return and take you in my arms.'

Agathe was totally at a loss to understand this strange letter. She was deeply hurt, but could not bear to be thought of as a hindrance. She wrote back telling him not to come, and the relationship ended there. Years later, both Brahms and Agathe gave their reasons. Agathe wrote a semi-autobiographical novel where she said of a fictional Brahms: 'He, like all geniuses, belonged to humanity . . . she could never have filled his life with her great love.'

Brahms, recalling the episode to the poet Widmann, obviously refers to the failure of his concerto:

At the time when I should have liked to marry, my music was either hissed in the concert rooms or at least received with icy coldness. Now for myself I could bear that quite well because I knew its worth, and that some day the tables would be turned. And when after such failures, I entered my lonely room I was not unhappy. On the contrary! But if at such moments I had had to meet the anxious, questioning eyes of a wife with the words 'another failure!' I could not have borne that . . . And if she had wanted to comfort me . . . a wife to pity her husband for his non-success – ugh! I cannot think what a hell that would have been, at least to me.

The house where Brahms lodged at Hamm, and of which he wrote: 'It is simply delightful to listen to the nightingales singing among budding branches.'

Even so, it is a strange excuse and may have been used to cover up an irresolution and timidity in his make-up which is not observable elsewhere.

Putting Agathe to the back of his mind, Brahms returned to Hamburg where he tried to pick up the threads of his career. He made important contacts in the Hamburg Philharmonic Orchestra including the conductor Karl Grädener; but although he had not published anything for five years, the failure of his concerto prevented him contacting publishers as he had originally intended. Instead he gave concerts of his works. The piano concerto was performed on 24 March in Hamburg, where it achieved some small measure of success, and another concert given by Brahms with Joachim and Stockhausen on 27 March included the first public performance of the orchestral Serenade No.1, which was also received with gratifying praise by the people of Hamburg.

Conditions at home grated on his nerves, however. Although the Brahms family were now living in a larger apartment in the *Fuhlentwiete*, thanks to Jakob's permanent position in the theatre orchestra and the money Johannes sent them when he could, and despite having his own room where he housed his growing collection of rare books, he wrote to Joachim at the time: 'I am living here as though I were in a kitchen.'

His father and mother had also begun to quarrel badly, abetted by his brother and sister. Years of privation and an age difference that became more obvious as they grew older, must all have played their part, and the atmosphere was tense and uncertain. Work was impossible under these conditions, and as spring approached he began to long for space and light and, above all, the sight of trees. Writing to Joachim, he admits: 'There are lovely rooms here outside the city gates so beautiful that I often look longingly at them.'

Then the opportunity arose to rent one. A pair of sisters, Betty and Marie Völcker, who had received lessons from Brahms in Hamburg, put him in touch with their aunt, Frau Dr Rösing, whose house in nearby Hamm had just such a room to rent. Brahms was soon installed there. Writing from his balcony to Dietrich, he enthused later: 'Everything is in blossom now . . . it is simply delightful to listen to the nightingales singing among budding branches.'

Here he taught, composed and involved himself with a local girls' choir whose members included the Völcker sisters. Writing to Clara about them, he said: 'I feel certain that you have enough youthful spirit to be amused by my Girls' Choir.' He enjoyed their company enormously and his irreverent sense of humour found expression in a set of mock rules he drew up for their conduct, written in a pompous officialese that must have satirised many a court pronouncement at Detmold.

During this happy period he composed much music for his choir: vocal quartets, part-songs including Ossian's *Fingal's Song* with horn and harp, the *Songs of Mary*, Op.22, and *Psalm 13*, Op.27. Dietrich, visiting Hamburg the following year, mentions outings he made to Hamm where a quartet drawn from the choir sang 'most delightfully in the neighbouring garden', and Clara Schumann, who had visited Brahms earlier, wrote in her diary of 'A delightful expedition to the Blankensee by steamer . . . we found the loveliest trees in the garden there and sang beneath them with Johannes conducting from a branch.'

There was undoubtedly an element of flirtatious libido in Brahms's dealings with these young girls, especially with the quartet made up of the Völcker sisters and their friends Laura Garbe and Marie Reuter. Brahms even playfully told his sister that Laura might soon become her sister-in-law. But his favourite was the Viennese girl Bertha Porubszky, who chattered on delightfully about Vienna and sang folk-songs of her native land, warming his heart to a less austere Germanic climate. Brahms told Joachim that through her, 'Vienna, which is, after all the musician's holy city, has taken on a double magic for me.'

Yet in all this he never committed himself wholeheartedly to anyone. His dealings with the girls of the Hamburg sailors' bars had left too deep a mark, and although he responded to pretty girls with fine voices on a sentimental level, worshipping them ideally as he had worshipped Clara, he always drew back at the moment of decision when the game of sex began to turn serious. So, we hear no more of Bertha until her marriage to Arthur Faber in Vienna shortly afterwards, and the composition of Brahms's popular *Cradle Song* – itself a variation on an Austrian folk-song – for their first child.

After the exceptionally pleasant summer of 1859 Brahms found Detmold more irksome than ever. He had outgrown a retreat that

Brahms's manuscript for the *Cradle Song*.

had once soothed his shattered nerves; he realised that he was simply marking time, and was ready to broaden his horizons. He hoped that he might in due course succeed Wilhelm Grund, the aged conductor of the Hamburg Philharmonic Orchestra and with this in mind he asked the prince if he might conduct orchestral works to gain experience. But the prince did not wish to offend his own resident conductor, the prickly August Kiel, and would only allow Brahms to conduct works that included a chorus with the orchestra. Brahms decided that he could no longer stand these petty intrigues, and when his term ended in January 1860 he declined to renew his contract.

He had had to put up with a great deal of humiliation, and the court was famous for its meanness. Clara, engaged to perform there the following February, wrote to Brahms on this matter:

I played there on three evenings in addition without getting a half-penny more. The princess sent me a bracelet. I believe it was one she had discarded in her youth, for it was so hideous that I could not wear it and . . . I sold it . . . in so doing discovered that it was filled with lead and zinc. It really is incredible!

And Brahms, who had been pleased to receive the first six volumes of the Bach definitive edition from the princess as a Christmas present, later discovered that subsequent volumes had been ordered in his name and that he had to pay for them as they appeared.

Altogether he was not sorry to leave, though it had been a fruitful autumn. He had composed a second orchestral work, the

47

Serenade in A major, Op.16, more intimate than the first but with the same relaxed flavour; he had begun a piano quartet in G minor and two sextets, the second of which includes the name Agathe as a theme in the Old German notation as some sort of retrospective atonement for his treatment of the girl. But he knew he had more important things to do than play court-lackey, and now set his sights firmly on the Hamburg appointment so dear to his heart.

Yet his first actions did nothing to further his career. Animosities had come to a head and Brahms charged in with a bull-like disregard for the consequences.

5 Caution

Although Robert Schumann had founded the *Neue Zeitschrift für Musik*, he had gradually moved away from it altogether until it had become a mouthpiece for the New German faction under its editor, Paul Brendel. So excluded were Schumann's ideas that Clara, Joachim and Brahms – those most associated with the late founder – were not even invited to its twenty-fifth anniversary celebrations at the end of 1859, and the aims of the New Germans were so established that in issue after issue they were confidently flaunted as the only relevant musical trend.

Brahms had become increasingly aware that the music he most admired and on which he based his artistic aims was, when not entirely ignored, certainly considered outmoded. Liszt and Wagner were the new gods. Referring to a performance of a work by Liszt in January 1860, Brahms had written to Clara: 'This plague will spread and spread. It will be sure to lengthen and deteriorate the donkeys' ears of the public and young composers.' So he decided to redress the balance by publishing a manifesto of protest.

The document was drawn up in January. Joachim was coerced into lending his support against his better judgement, and they both searched for other important signatories. Many leading musicians promised to sign, including Niels Gade, the leading Danish composer, but due to some slip-up, or maybe a doubtful journalistic scoop, the manifesto was published prematurely with only four signatures in the Berlin *Echo*. As such, it must rank as one of the worst public relations exercises on record. The text ran:

The undersigned have regretfully followed the aims of a certain faction whose journal is Brendel's *Zeitschrift für Musik*.

The above-mentioned magazine continually states that serious musicians are basically in agreement with the cause it espouses, that they see work of artistic merit in the creations of the leaders of this faction and that, all in all, especially in North Germany, the arguments for and against the so-called 'music of the future' are settled in their favour.

The undersigned consider it their duty to protest against such falsification of the facts, and state that, as far as they are concerned, they do not recognise Brendel's cause and consider the products of the leaders and followers of the New German school, which partly uphold this cause and partly enforce new and unknown theories, to be contrary to the innermost spirit of music and to be strongly deplored and condemned.

JOHANNES BRAHMS
JOSEPH JOACHIM
JULIUS OTTO GRIMM
BERNHARD SCHOLZ

Richard Wagner, Brahms's arch-rival, a leading composer of the New German school.

As artistic manifestos go, this one is no vaguer than many, but it must have caused gales of laughter in the New German camp. Wagner replied in the *Zeitschrift* in typical vein, with a vicious article against Jews in music by way of a swipe at Joachim who was partly Jewish, and he may have been responsible for the satirical mock-letters of ridicule and protest which also appeared in the May issue heralding, among other things, this new 'brotherhood for the advancement of monotonous and tiresome music'.

Joachim, being the best known of the four, naturally received most of the backlash, but Brahms was the one most profoundly affected by this monumental *gaffe*. He suddenly realised how isolated and vulnerable he was in faction-ridden musical Germany and knew that, having declared himself the guardian of the true inner spirit of music, he must from then on live up to that ideal. We do not know what bonfires of works followed this sudden realisation, but we do know that from then on the 'young Kreisler' took a back seat and the romantic Brahms became more close-mouthed, resolving to channel his passion and energy more rigidly through classical and pre-classical forms. He was just twenty-six.

Yet Brahms had been moving against this aspect of his nature since the Schumann episode. Now he saw more clearly the need for balance in his life as much as in his art. He saw that the Romantic movement, with which he had flirted, had an element of hysteria bordering on the schizophrenic: it was obsessed with nervous exaltation, unearthly bliss and tragic death; its prose was littered with exclamation marks, its art with morbid or wild scenarios, its music with neurotic changes of tempo. The casualty list of madness and suicide was enormous: it was almost fashionable. Most significantly for Brahms, it was Schumann who had sustained the most damaging effects of the movement, and whose elations and despairs had ended in the characteristically Romantic way, with attempted suicide and an asylum.

The continual influence of Clara was also a sobering one. Whatever her virtues as an artist, wife and mother, she most definitely lacked a sense of humour, and the caution she had exercised over her husband was now turned on Brahms. Yet, if he became more critical and reserved from this point, self-assurance gradually emerged and he soon grew surer of his strength.

Dietrich, unaware of these internal struggles, played host to Brahms in Bonn that spring. He had married in the previous year and had recently been appointed director of the town's subscription concerts. The Dietrichs were both delighted to receive Brahms as their first house-guest, and Albert wrote of the occasion:

After six years of silence, Brahms had brought with him a number of new and splendid compositions to which we were now introduced. They were the Serenades in A major and D major, the *Ave Maria* for female chorus, the *Funeral Hymn* . . . songs and romances and the Piano Concerto . . . He had also written a choral mass . . . which, however, was not published.

While in Bonn, Brahms met the publisher Fritz Simrock who offered to publish his Second Serenade and First Sextet. Over the years, a close friendship was to grow up between the two men.

Brahms spent happy hours music-making at 'one of the most beautiful villas on the opposite side of the Rhine', home of the cultured Kyllman family and, after sponsoring Dietrich's son at his christening, he returned to Hamburg to do battle for his cause.

Despite writing that 'a man with so few ties as I have can easily disappear overnight', Brahms was to remain in Hamburg at his retreat in Hamm for the better part of the next two years, dividing his time between teaching, the concert platform and a strict composing régime. But he did find another base in Switzerland. A pupil of Schumann's, Theodor Kirchner, invited him to stay at the small town of Wintherthur, where he was resident organist. Writing of the town early in 1853, Hans von Bülow had said:

Wintherthur . . . thanks to the artistic efforts of such intelligent and gifted men as Theodor Kirchner . . . can boast of a more real and intense musical life than that which Munich . . . will ever attain.

Brahms visited Kirchner there first in 1860 and then many times during the next two years, appearing as soloist in his own works as well as accompanying Kirchner and Friedrich Hegar – a young violinist who was to be a close friend for many years. He also found a new publisher in the town, Rieter-Biedermann, who published his Piano Concerto in 1861. Brahms eventually grew very fond of Switzerland, where he was always to be assured of a sympathetic hearing for his music.

In the spring of 1861 Dietrich paid a return visit to Brahms and stayed with his parents in Hamburg. 'I was surprised at the extent of his library . . . there were some remarkable old things', he reported. Brahms showed him his boxes of tin soldiers 'saying he could not bring himself to part with such dear mementoes of childhood'. Brahms, of course, was in Hamm where Dietrich spent the better part of the day. Here Brahms showed him his latest compositions. 'Contrary to his custom' he played through the sketches of a new piano quartet — the one in A major, Op.25 — which he later dedicated to Frau Rösing. Dietrich considered it 'one of his most beautiful works'.

Dietrich had taken up another appointment as music director to the court of the Duke of Oldenburg, and Brahms appeared there the following year as soloist in Beethoven's Fourth Piano Concerto which was 'simply perfect' according to Dietrich, although 'a laurel wreath which had been hung over his chair, he modestly laid underneath the pianoforte'.

He had also brought a new work with him in which his new resolve to temper passion with intellect can be most strongly discerned. As he played his monumental piano Variations and Fugue on a theme of Handel, Op.24, to the orchestra at a rehearsal the night before the concert, they were delighted, Dietrich finding

Cologne: Brahms was a
frequent visitor to its
prestigious music festival.

the Variations 'wonderfully beautiful and full of true genius'.
During this visit, Dietrich records, Brahms 'came in contact with
many people who all appreciated his earnestness as well as the
humour which frequently showed itself in his remarks'.

The works he had produced by the end of the year are marked
with a new sense of craftsmanship and yet remain as lyrical as
anything he had written to date. Apart from the two piano quartets
and the Handel Variations, he had also completed his two sextets
and a sonata for two pianos in F minor which, with tireless self-
discipline, he had already arranged as a string quintet before it
would achieve the artistically satisfying form of piano quintet. He
was still reluctant to publish even these efforts, only the Handel
Variations being brought out by Breitkopf and Härtel. He was
only too aware of the the artistic credo he had published.

Musical festivals are always a pleasant diversion for a dedicated
composer, and Brahms was always present at those staged along
the Rhine. After visiting the Düsseldorf Festival in June 1862,
Dietrich and he set off to nearby Münster am Stein to spend the
summer months near Clara Schumann and her children, who were
taking a health cure in the spa town. Brahms composed some of his
Magelone songs there; Dietrich called them 'the loveliest songs he
had yet written' and recorded that Brahms showed him the first
movement of a symphony in C minor, 'which only appeared much
later and with considerable alterations'. In fact, the signatory of

the manifesto would not reveal this masterpiece for another fourteen years.

At a festival in Cologne that year Brahms met another of the lady singers who so attracted him. Luise Dustmann-Meyer, like Bertha, came from Vienna and the vivacity with which she praised her native city sparked off a dormant desire to visit the musical capital of the south. In September, Brahms decided. A few days later he was sitting at a café table in the legendary 'musician's holy city' itself.

6 Vienna

> I have made a move and am living here ten paces from the Prater and can drink my wine where Beethoven used to drink his.

So Brahms wrote enthusiastically to Otto Grimm from Vienna. Seat of the Habsburgs, the city that so impressed him was the capital of one the longest-lived European empires. Imperial and royal, it embraced not only Austria and Hungary but also large portions of modern Czechoslovakia, Poland, Italy and the Balkans; bordering the emerging Germany of the North, and Russia and Turkey to the south and east, its centre was the meeting-place of all these exotic influences. But for all its imperial swagger and the attempts of its emperor Franz Joseph II to vie with Prussia for hegemony over a unified German empire, it was really a politically exhausted experiment in multi-nationalism that lacked the single-minded drive of the North. Yet as it declined as a viable political entity its creative dynamo hummed and, in the fifty years of life it had left, it was to become the centre of European art, thought and music.

Brahms, from the puritan North, had never encountered such warmth and vivacity. The teeming boulevards, lamp-lit cafés with gypsy bands, and the Prater pleasure gardens alone would have captivated him, but its sheer musicality was intoxication itself. Here those predecessors he most admired – Haydn, Mozart, Beethoven and Schubert – had lived and died, and their influence was still felt. Apart from such official bodies as the court opera, semi-official bands of enthusiasts such as the Vienna Philharmonic Society which regularly performed orchestral and choral works, and the *Singakademie* with its fine tradition of church music, there were numerous chamber groups, many fine soloists and, on the lighter side which the Viennese adored more than anything, the lilt of the waltz vendors, chief among them being the renowned family Strauss.

Vienna knew virtually nothing of Brahms and he had to seek a reputation all over again. In this he was fortunate for the city contained many old friends, including Luise, now returned to her home and rehearsing Isolde in *Tristan and Isolde*; Bertha Faber and her husband Arthur also welcomed the young composer, and he re-established contact with Karl Grädener who had left Hamburg to teach at the Vienna Conservatoire. Through them, Brahms met the leading lights of the Viennese musical circle. The pianist Julius Epstein opened most doors for him, and he was soon friendly with the fussy little Beethoven scholar Gustav Nottebohm, the composer Peter Cornelius and the pianist Karl Tausig. He had encountered both Cornelius and Tausig at the Villa Altenberg. They were, of course, New Germans, but so free of prejudice that they appreciated Brahms's gifts without reservation. The feeling was mutual and Brahms was particularly impressed by Tausig, writing to Clara: 'He is really a remarkable little fellow and a very exceptional pianist.'

Tausig's virtuosity inspired Brahms to produce the stunningly complex two books of Variations on the well-tried Paganini theme, Op.35, which he completed in 1863, evoking from Clara the complaint that they were 'Witch Variations', too difficult for frail lady pianists of her ilk. All these musicians had a great zest for the good things of Viennese life and were all to become life-long friends of Brahms. Nottebohm, especially, was the butt of Brahms's none too subtle humour. On one occasion Brahms faked a Beethoven sketch and bribed a chip-vendor in the Prater to wrap Nottebohm's chips in it. As the bogus prize was revealed chip by chip, Nottebohm went into an ecstasy of discovery, only to be rudely deflated a few moments later by the guffaws of Brahms and his companions.

His first venue as a composer was Epstein's house. Mozart had composed his *Marriage of Figaro* there and Brahms must have been delighted when Vienna's pre-eminent quartet, the

Vienna, 'the musicians holy city'.

55

Promenade concert at the Kursaal, Vienna. Brahms was intoxicated by the city's musicality.

Hellmesberger, arrived to join him in a private performance of his piano quartets in G minor and A major. Afterwards their leader turned to Brahms and rapturously declared him to be Beethoven's heir – a tag that pleased him at the time, though it was later to cause him a great deal of annoyance. The quartet went on to perform the A major quartet at the Vienna Philharmonic Society on 29 November, a concert where Brahms also performed his Handel Variations, exciting a great deal of interest among the musical public, so that Brahms could write to his parents:

I was so happy yesterday, my concert was a great success, more so than I had hoped . . . I played as though I were relaxing at home with friends, and the public is certainly more stimulating than ours. You should have seen their concentration, and heard the applause afterwards!

Yet even as Vienna listened with approval, Hamburg turned a cold shoulder. Brahms received news that his friend Stockhausen had gained the coveted post of director of the Hamburg Philharmonic Orchestra. The hope of that position had been Brahms's chief focus for two years, and to find that he had marked time in Hamburg in vain was a bitter disappointment to him. He wrote to Clara on 18 November:

It represents a much sadder event for me than you can imagine . . . I suppose I am a little bit old-fashioned, in any case I certainly am so in this

Eduard Hanslick, Vienna's most influential critic, who became a firm supporter of Brahms.

Johann Herbeck, conductor of the Vienna Philharmonic Society concerts.

respect, that I am not a cosmopolitan but am as attached to my native town as I might be to my mother . . . How rare it is for one of us to find a permanent niche and how glad I should have been to find mine in my native town. Happy as I am here with many beautiful things to gladden my heart, I nevertheless feel, and shall always feel, that I am a stranger and can have no peace . . . You know that, as a general rule, what our fellow-citizens like best is to be rid of us and to allow us to flit about in the desert waste of the world. And yet one wants to be bound, and to acquire all that makes life worth living. One is naturally frightened by the thought of solitude.

Joachim was incredulous and wrote to Avé Lallement, who had worked hard for Brahms as a member of the selection committee:

If every one of you . . . had shown some confidence and friendship . . . instead of revealing arrogance and distrust, it would have helped iron out some of his personality difficulties . . . He is bound to grow more bitter when he finds himself isolated all the time.

His reception in Vienna was some consolation. On 6 January 1863 he played his third piano sonata and accompanied some of his songs at a concert which both Wagner and the influential critic Eduard Hanslick attended. Hanslick was guarded in his appraisal although he enjoyed the slow movement of the sonata, whereas Wagner was too self-centred to venture any opinion at all, despite the help Brahms had given by copying out parts of *Die Meistersinger* for concert performance during his stay.

March saw the performance of Brahms's two orchestral works: the first Serenade was performed at one of Johann Herbeck's concerts at the Philharmonic Society, and Otto Dessoff conducted the second Serenade shortly afterwards. Following these performances, the scales fell from Hanslick's eyes and he became an unwavering supporter who went on to lend his considerable critical support to Brahms for the rest of his career.

On 26 March Brahms was still enthusiastically praising Vienna. In a letter to his friend Adolf Schubring he wrote:

I have spent the whole winter here, very much at a loose end, but rather enjoyably and cheerfully. I regret above all things that I didn't know Vienna before. The gaiety of the town, the beauty of the surroundings, the sympathetic and vivacious public, how stimulating these are to the artist! In addition we have in particular the sacred memory of the great musicians whose lives and work are brought daily to our minds. In the case of Schubert especially one has the impression of his being still alive. Again and again one meets people who talk of him as a good friend; again and again one comes across new works, the existence of which was unknown and which are so untouched that one can scrape the very writing sand off them.

Clearly his love of browsing among antiquities could receive no greater thrill than this, and when he was introduced to Spina, who published two of his choral works, he was lent Schubert's unfinished cantata *Lazarus*, where the writing sand was indeed

Franz Schubert, of whom Brahms wrote: 'One has the impression of his being still alive.'

still thickly encrusted. This he carefully preserved as a souvenir in a box kept specially for the purpose. Sending Dietrich excerpts he had copied from the score, he wrote: 'If I could send you the whole, you would be delighted at such sweetness!'

One final concert,which included choruses for female voices, on 10 April rounded off Brahms's visit. He lingered in Vienna until May then left for Hanover to join Joachim, who was neither free nor lonely any longer. He had married.

Joachim's wife was the contralto Amalie Weiss. Brahms fell in love with her voice when he heard her in Gluck's *Orpheus and Eurydice*. Writing to Dietrich, he said: 'The new bride has quite charmed me, first when we were strolling gaily through the wood, and then by her quiet dignity in the role of Orpheus!'

Although he approved, his own misgivings about marriage in relation to what he saw as his mission as a composer had surfaced in a confused manner when he wrote from Vienna congratulating the pair:

You lucky dog! What else can I write but some such exclamation? . . . Nobody will appreciate your good fortune more than I do just now, when your letter found me in just the mood to be deeply affected. For I cannot leave off wondering whether I, who had better be on my guard against other dreams, am to enjoy everything here but the One, or to go home and give up everything else. Now you break in on these thoughts and boldly pluck for yourself the finest and ripest apples of Paradise . . .

Was Brahms happy in spite of his freedom, as his personal motto still implied? His thinking is obscurely expressed and was to become even more obscure as the years passed, causing many open breaches with his closest friends. It cannot be blamed on shyness, for an even more diffident youth had written to Joachim of his dearest wishes and had told Clara that he adored her so entirely that he would have to set her in gold. His thinking on this one subject was now so introspective, so involved with spurious wishes and unattainable ideals, that he could not communicate it even to the most sympathetic people he knew. Much of the melancholy that increasingly darkened what remained of a sunny disposition must be traced back to these days.

While staying in Hanover, Brahms received confirmation of Vienna's opinion of his gifts: he was invited to return there in the autumn as director of the *Singakademie* for its winter season. It was a heaven-sent opportunity for someone who so obviously loved choral singing and the ancient music that this choir specialised in, but he felt the burden of inexperience, as is shown in this letter to Dietrich written at the time:

I should very much like to ask you to give me some information that will be of use to me there . . . I do not really know what to ask you, and yet am extremely shy of making my first attempt in this line at Vienna of all places . . . Altogether, I beg you, as an experienced and highly learned conductor, to give me your advice.

He vacillated, but accepted. Then, leaving the newly wed Joachims to their bliss, perhaps feeling that the doors of his early enthusiastic friendship were now almost closed, Brahms went to spend the interim with his parents in Hamburg. But there was little peace to be found there. His parents' quarrels were virtually open war. The apartment was their battlefield. His sister had formed an alliance with his seventy-four-year-old mother against his still youthful middle-aged father, and his brother was simply a neutral observer. Brahms preferred to retire to lodgings at the nearby Blankensee, where he found enough peace and quiet to begin a cantata based on Goethe's medieval romance, *Rinaldo*, though he did make occasional sorties to his parents' to try and effect a truce. His thirtieth birthday was spent in this atmosphere of rancour, from which he eventually escaped to Oldenburg. Here he was able to relax with the Dietrichs. 'Those were merry days! How much we laughed!' Dietrich wrote. But Brahms had confided his distress to Clara, who had replied:

I was sorry to see that your letter was not at all cheerful and that dear old Hamburg no longer pleased you. And yet I foresaw that this would be the

Lichtenthal, where Clara Schumann owned a holiday house and Brahms often stayed in the summer months.

case when once you had learned to know the life of Vienna which . . . is more stimulating.

Brahms moved on from Oldenburg to join Clara at her new holiday home in Lichtenthal near Baden-Baden. Here he spent several weeks, enjoying walks in the nearby woods and preparing himself for Vienna, before leaving on 28 September to take up his new appointment.

*   *   *   *

'You have unquestionably won the most perfect laurels. I really revelled – each piece was more beautiful than the last,' Cornelius wrote to Brahms after the first concert, given on 15 November. The works performed then clearly reflected Brahms's interests: Bach and Beethoven cantatas, Schumann's *Requiem für Mignon* and folk-song arrangements by himself. Later concerts included works by Gabrielli and Schütz, Bach's *Christmas Oratorio* and even English Elizabethan madrigals. Writing to Clara, Brahms reported:

The *Christmas Oratorio* went excellently at our third concert . . . The choir and I enjoyed it at all events, but a work of Bach's has a difficult time with the critics here. Hanslick must have suffered the pains of the

60

Johann Sebastian Bach. Brahms devoted a large part of his life to making Bach's music better known.

damned during the week, for two days afterwards Herbeck's *St. John Passion* was performed.

Although Vienna respected the earnest artistry of Brahms's programming, it did not generally share Cornelius's enthusiasm. It disliked gloom, and even the *Singakademie* choir itself joked: 'When Brahms is in really high spirits, he gets us to sing *The Grave is my Joy!*'

But it was an eventful season in other ways. The First String Sextet in B flat, Op.18, was warmly applauded when Hellmesberger performed it in December, and Brahms moved in a bright social round, even narrowly missing matrimony. He had met Ottolie Hauer at the house of Clara's friends, the Astens. She was a member of yet another of his small ladies' choirs, and so excelled in his songs that Brahms eventually lost his head and proposed to her on Christmas Day. He later told Clara: 'She was a very pretty girl with whom, God knows, I might have made a fool of myself if, as luck would have it, someone had not snatched her up.'

That 'someone' was Dr Edward Ebner, and Ottolie had accepted his proposal only a few hours earlier. This did not sour Brahms, who soon converted his feelings into yet another friendship with an object of former sentimental passion. It is also possible that he had unconsciously known about Edward Ebner, and had merely gone through the forms of a proposal as a sop to his barely clarified desires for domesticity.

A few weeks later another singer fascinated Brahms. Elisabeth von Stockhausen took lessons from him briefly, and one account says he was overwhelmed by her wit and brilliant magnetism, for she was certainly a positive and very beautiful girl. Yet if Brahms was overwhelmed at first, he soon showed symptoms of extreme fright and quickly palmed her off on Julius Epstein. After teaching her for a while, he too declared that it was impossible not to fall in love with her. Elisabeth flashed into both their lives only to disappear with mercurial speed. When she reappeared in Brahms's view eleven years later, it was to be on much more manageable terms.

Apart from fending off the ladies Brahms had also found time to visit his greatest rival. Cornelius and Tausig took him to meet their idol Richard Wagner at nearby Penzing on 6 February. The two composers spent a cordial evening together, though Brahms must have been as instinctively repelled by Wagner's taste for silk and velvet suits, his conceit and love of luxury, as he had been repelled by Liszt's palatial surroundings. Brahms played his Handel Variations to Wagner, who was so impressed that he grudgingly conceded: 'One sees what may still be achieved with the old forms in the hand of someone who knows what to do with them.' Although this was high praise from such an egoist, the evening did not bear fruit and they never met again. Wagner was, as always, pursued by creditors and made his escape to Bavaria the following

61

month. There this former revolutionary spent two years reinforcing the candy-floss fantasies of King Ludwig II, maddest of the dotty Bavarian dynasty. Although Brahms continued to respect Wagner's music all his life, Wagner directed many vicious attacks on Brahms in later years, raving among other things that he was a 'Jewish czardas player' (anyone who displeased Wagner was instantly a Jew).

The final concert of the *Singakademie* season took place in April 1864. This consisted entirely of Brahms's own choral pieces and was applauded unreservedly. Brahms, however, was only too aware that his directorship had been a lukewarm success, and as the administration bored him, he declined their formal offer of another three years in the post, excusing himself in a letter to his friend Adolph Schubring:

While in any other city, a regular position is desirable, in Vienna one lives better without it. The many interesting people, the libraries, the Burgtheater, the picture galleries, all these give me enough to do and enjoy outside my own room.

But despite his confidence, he was still unsure of his direction, as he had written to Dietrich:

It is possible that I shall not remain here much longer; in that case I should go to Hamburg and see you soon. It is more difficult to know where to go to when one is neither held back nor pushed forward.

In the end, he decided to return to Hamburg, although he soon regretted his decision. There was uneasiness on two fronts. Austria and Prussia were at war with Denmark in nearby Schleswig-Holstein – a preliminary arm-lock in Bismarck's control of northern Germany – and there were also domestic battles raging once more. An event that would have been an excuse for family rejoicing in the old days, with much drinking of egg-nog, was now the cause of renewed dissent. Stockhausen had appointed Brahms's father to the back desk of the Hamburg Philharmonic, and this required much more practice at home on the double bass. The aged mother and the sister, who suffered so greatly with headaches, were finally driven frantic by its mournful grumblings and had forced Jakob Brahms to practise in the attic.

Clara consoled Johannes: 'That you, who have been longing for a whole year to join your people should light upon just this unhappy juncture of affairs grieves me very much.' Brahms tried reconciliation, but saw that there was now an irreversible breach in his parents' relationship. Bowing sadly to the inevitable, he found a room in the *Grosse Bleicher* for his father. His mother and sister remained together in the old apartment for the time being, and Brahms promised to help maintain the two establishments despite his erratic income which was based almost entirely on teaching and the odd concert receipt.

Having settled the ruins of his family as best he could, Brahms left war-scared Hamburg for the peace of Clara's Lichtenthal retreat, although he continued writing letters to his family with desperate diplomacy. On hearing in November that his mother and sister had moved to an apartment with a garden where they still kept a room for him, Brahms wrote to his father:

That mother and Elise have reserved a room for me would please me indeed if I could think that you would occupy it frequently . . . You can often take your afternoon nap in the company of my books . . . Do your best, even if this should be unpleasant at times. Help them with the moving, and don't let yourself be driven away; the time will come when she and all of us will thank you . . .

But it was no use. His father and mother would never again exchange even formal courtesies.

Lichtenthal was a sympathetic base for the wanderer now that Hamburg was growing remote. In the sophisticated spa of Baden-Baden nearby, among the many famous and titled people who gathered to sip its waters, Brahms met several new friends. There was Johann Strauss II, whose music he admired so much that he later said he would give all his works to have written the *Blue Danube* waltz. He also enjoyed the company of Anselm Feuerbach, leader of the Deutsch-Römer school of art whose concern with the spirit of Roman classicism, expressed with

Baden-Baden, the fashionable spa where Brahms met Johann Strauss.

almost Pre-Raphaelite clarity, struck a sympathetic chord in Brahms. At this time he also found he had much in common with the humane and tolerant Russian novelist Turgenev who was travelling in Europe with his singer friend Pauline Viardot. Turgenev even suggested collaborating on an opera with Brahms. Brahms had just finished the cantata *Rinaldo*, Op.50, which shows strong dramatic leanings, but, although he was clearly interested, he might have realised his own limitations in this field, and when they parted he did not pursue the project further. Nearby Karlsruhe also provided stimulus. Brahms met the conductor of the opera house there, Herman Levi, who so fell under Brahms's influence that he immediately offered to perform any orchestral works Brahms might offer him, and was to become a firm champion of his cause from then on.

In these civilised surroundings Brahms put the finishing touches to his Piano Quintet in F minor, Op.34, arranged from the two-piano sonata of 1861, then, restless as always, he returned to Vienna, took shabby lodgings and moved once more among the 'many interesting people' of the metropolis. Inspired by their infectious gaiety, and hoping to emulate Johann Strauss, he completed his first collection of Waltzes, Op.39, for piano duet; but at Christmas his thoughts turned once more to his estranged family and he wrote unhappily to his father: 'Aren't you going to spend one evening with mother?' But the stubborn Holsteiner would not go and then, suddenly, it was too late. On 2 February 1865 Fritz Brahms sent a telegram to his brother: 'Come at once if you want to see mother again.'

Brahms left for Hamburg immediately, but before he arrived his mother died of a stroke.

7 Restlessness and Recognition

Brahms had treasured his mother with a deeper sense of pure love than he bore for any other member of his family. Although he adored both his parents, it was his mother who had understood him best and whose letters shone with the sympathy and firm practical advice that had been his mainstay as he sought recognition for his gifts. It was she who had voiced the family's pride when he achieved his first successes, and she who had made their poor apartment bright for his triumphant returns. He shouldered the burden of the arrangements, hiding his grief as best he could. Writing to Clara on 6 February, he grieved:

We buried her yesterday at one o'clock. She had not changed at all and looked as sweet and kind as when she was alive. Everything that could possibly be done to comfort one for such a loss was done, particularly for my sister.

His sister went to lodge with Brahms's former tutor, Cossel, and his family. Brahms promised to help support her in her separate existence, saw that his father was reasonably settled in his lodgings, then returned to Vienna. There on 20 February he unburdened himself in a letter to Clara:

Time changes everything for better or worse. It does not so much change as it builds up and develops, and thus when once this sad year is over I shall begin to miss my dear good mother ever more and more . . . The one comforting feature about our loss is that it ended a relationship which really could only have become sadder with the years.

Slowly, his grief emerged as music. After Schumann's death he had conceived a design for a requiem based not on the usual Latin mass for the dead, but on texts from Luther's translation of the Bible, probably taking his cue from Schubert's German masses. Now he returned to the project, using the slow movement he had written for the symphony that never appeared as a threnody to the words 'All flesh is as grass', and laying out sketches for another five movements to complement it emotionally.

Brahms was no longer a religious man in the strict sense of the term. Before this event, he had subjected his Lutheran upbringing to the acid test of intellect and rejected vast areas of belief. What he had retained was an approval of Christian ethics in the conduct of life and a profound respect for its literature. Biblical images celebrated all the seasons of man, and he sifted them finely so that

they would be a reflection of his love of life rather than a conventionally religious fear of death and redemption through suffering. He later told Reinthaler, the pious organist at Bremen cathedral who prepared the first full performance, that he would have liked to call it a 'Requiem of Mankind', having 'quite consciously avoided passages like . . . "For God so loved the world that He gave His only begotten son, that whoso believeth in Him should not perish but have everlasting life". Although I have used others because as a musician I needed them and because I could not deprive my honoured poets of their effects . . .'

He decided to call this humanist's liturgy of mourning and comfort through tradition *A German Requiem*, a title reflecting the vernacular texts rather than anything more narrowly national.

Work on this massive composition continued for at least another year, but several other important works were written or completed in 1865. Staying at Lichtenthal that summer, he produced the Horn Trio in E flat major, Op.40, part of which was inspired by seeing the sunrise in the woods, as he later told Dietrich, showing him the exact spot where he had stood. Brahms's romantic evocation of the woods that had inspired him was even carried over to the choice of horn, which he specified should be the *Waldhorn*, or valveless natural horn. Such is the calm melancholy of the music that the slow movement is often regarded as an elegy for his mother. He also completed a work that had been lying beside him for three years. The First Cello Sonata in E minor, Op.38, was frankly experimental, an attempt to

Zurich: Brahms's music found especial favour in Switzerland.

combine warm melody with the contrapuntal play of Bach and the poise of the eighteenth century.

While staying at Lichtenthal he received a letter from his father, which was a rare enough event to cause Brahms some anxiety. He wrote:

I hope you won't hold it against me if I tell you that I am thinking of marrying again . . . My choice has fallen on a woman who, though of course she won't make you forget your mother, has every right to your respect . . . She is a widow . . . forty-one years old.

Brahms must have been shocked at the suddenness of the engagement and concerned that once more his father seemed oblivious to age differences. He set off for Hamburg immediately, but when he met the widow in question his fears were allayed. Caroline Schnack had run the restaurant where the lonely Jakob Brahms had taken his meals, and the relationship that had developed seems a clear case of winning a man's heart through his stomach. She was indeed as proportionally young to his father as his mother had been old, but she was kind and positive and clearly

67

Theodor Billroth, surgeon and musician, who often tried out Brahms's compositions with him in two-piano transcriptions.

loved Jakob. Brahms approved and was pleased that at least one emotional weight had been lifted from his back. The two were married in March the following year and the union proved a very happy one indeed.

After seeing his father settled, the old restlessness came over Brahms. He was also impecunious and needed the external stimulus of the concert hall as much to fill his pocket as to occupy his thoughts. He returned to the old round of recital tours. On 9 November he performed his Piano Concerto in D minor, with Levi conducting, at Mannheim, and was gratified to find it acclaimed as the masterpiece he knew it to be. He followed this with a tour of Switzerland, that was equally successful. Staying in Winterthur and Zurich, he renewed his acquaintance with Hegar and met the surgeon and amateur musician Theodor Billroth, who was to become one of his closest friends. He also grew friendly with the photographer Julius Allgeyer and Mathilde Wesendonck, another of Wagner's conquests whose civilised refinement had inspired him to write *Tristan und Isolde* before she decided to stay with her husband in the end. At her home he studied the scores of *Das Rheingold* and *Die Walküre*, neither of which had been performed, and was duly impressed. Writing to Clara in December, he told her:

I had a very restless time . . . I brought about 1800 francs back with me . . . After my first concert in Zurich when I played my D major serenade, one or two musical friends (particularly Dr Lübke, Professor Billroth and Wesendonck) organised a private concert . . . so that I might hear my concerto and A major serenade . . . The whole affair was very gratifying.

In Winterthur the poet J. V. Widmann sat in the audience unaware that the genius playing for him would become one of his closest friends in later years. 'The total effect was of consummate strength,' Widmann wrote of Brahms's performance, 'both physical and moral.'

Returning to North Germany in December, he was welcomed at Detmold as a master by the amiable princess, and permitted a performance of his Horn Trio to take place at one of the prince's chamber concerts. Julius Allgeyer had invited Brahms to stay at his house in Karlsruhe, and Brahms took up the invitation in the New Year, staying there until April. This respite from his constant travelling allowed him enough time to finish the *Requiem*.

After the effort of producing his masterpiece, his immediate reaction was, as usual, one of caution. He put the work away to allow time to see it objectively, and returned to Switzerland to spend the summer at Zurich with his new friends. During his stay there he composed the bulk of a string quartet in C minor, the first he allowed to survive, having by his own admission destroyed 'a score' of quartets before this. But the Beethoven comparison still terrified him and he hid the work for another seven years.

He remained in Switzerland all summer. North Germany was suddenly unsafe. Bismarck had invaded Hanover, Hesse and Saxony, and Vienna was out of the question too. Brahms, who had watched Bismarck's unification policies with approval and even carried a copy of his speeches in his travelling-bag, would have been unwelcome there, for soon after Bismarck had defeated and absorbed the three North German states he invaded Austria, moving swiftly to defeat its imperial army at Königgratz on 3 July.

Brahms was, however, uneasy, regarding these battles as a civil war between brother Germans, though it helped to consolidate the dream of a united Germany, which Brahms as a patriot applauded wholeheartedly. By the end of July the conflict was virtually over and Brahms was free to travel again. He went straight to Lichtenthal, where he stayed near Clara. In the autumn, they visited the Dietrichs at Oldenburg, Dietrich writing: 'Even the breakfast hour was interesting and, thanks to Brahms's high spirits, merry! How enjoyable and cosy were the evenings!' Brahms had brought his first set of Hungarian Dances, arranged for four hands, and he and Clara 'played them at sight with such fire and brilliancy that it was followed by a general burst of enthusiasm'.

The war had left Joachim at a loose end now that the court of Hanover no longer existed, and he joined Brahms in October. The two immediately set off on a recital tour of Switzerland, which was a great success. In December, with the dust of war settled, Joachim returned to Hanover and Brahms went on to Vienna to join Billroth, who had recently been appointed director of the Surgical Institute there.

Brahms spent Christmas with Bertha Faber and her family and, finding that his North German background was not resented in view of recent events, remained there into the spring. In March and April, after playing his Handel and Paganini Variations at public concerts, (reporting to his father that 'the evenings went off splendidly'), he was rejoined by Joachim and they set off on another concert tour round Austria and as far as Budapest. It was Brahms's first visit to the twin capital of the Austro-Hungarian empire, but as early as 1856 he had followed Clara's accounts of her visits to Hungary with envy: 'I have often wanted to hear the gypsies playing. I should like to study and remember them, noting their melodies.'

Now he was able to hear the real thing and no doubt collected more themes to be used in his second set of Hungarian Dances. The tour was such a success that Brahms found he had more money than he needed. He decided to invite his father to visit him in Vienna for a summer holiday.

Although Jakob had spent nearly forty years in Hamburg without once stepping outside, a sudden urge to travel had overcome him after his second marriage. He had already visited his home village and was now delighted to accept his son's invitation to travel further south. When he arrived he fell in love

Budapest: Brahms wrote to Clara, 'I have often wanted to hear the gypsies playing'.

with Vienna, and Brahms was so childishly pleased to have the old man with him that he immediately wanted to show him everything and introduce him to everyone he knew. Friends and colleagues alike were delighted by the old musician's homely ways and he saw all the sights, even, as Brahms recounted in a letter to Joachim, the 'visiting Turkish pasha' and the Austrian emperor with the French emperor Napoleon III, who had arrived in Vienna to spin yet another web of intrigue with the Habsburgs. They did not stop in the city. Brahms insisted on shepherding his easy-going parent round his favourite mountains and, with the cellist Joseph Gänsbacher, they toured Styria, stopping in Mürzzuschlag, then moved on to the Salzkammergut region. Jakob enjoyed the holiday immensely, and when he returned to Hamburg he never stopped talking about it. He wrote to his son:

You can imagine how many people envy me. Of course, I exaggerate properly; I tell them I've climbed right to the top of the Schlafberg, but I don't tell them I rode on horseback three quarters of the way.

And Brahms wrote to Dietrich: 'Just imagine what a treat it was to me to see my father's pleasure, he who had never seen a mountain.'

Refreshed after this break, Brahms turned his attention to the *Requiem* once more. Herbeck had offered to try out the first three movements on 1 December at one of the Philharmonic Society

70

Programme for the first performance of the German Requiem in its three-movement version at Herbeck's Philharmonic Society concerts.

concerts, but when the day came he proved unsuitable for the task. The work had been under-rehearsed and in the final fugue of the third movement the tympanist drowned the choir and orchestra. The work added to Brahms's reputation as a purveyor of gloom among the Viennese, and in its truncated form very few appreciated its subtle originality. Hanslick reported that there was 'unanimous applause' despite these deficiencies, although he deplored the behaviour of 'half a dozen bald-headed fanatics of the old school' who hissed and later tried to assault one of Brahms's supporters. The second half of the concert consisted of a selection of Schubert's *Rosamunde* incidental music which must have thrown the *Requiem* movements into even more bizarre relief.

Brahms was untroubled by this semi-fiasco. Clara had written, on receiving the piano arrangement of the work, that it had given her 'unspeakable joy', and he knew that Dietrich had arranged for

71

the first official performance to be carefully rehearsed by Reinthaler for Good Friday in Bremen Cathedral the following year. After spending Chistmas in Vienna, Brahms visited Bremen where he adjusted the tympanist's part and left the work in Reinthaler's capable hands.

He then stopped off in Hamburg to visit his family. Writing an account of his visit to Clara, he voiced his latest anxiety:

I am living with my father and up to the present have quite enjoyed sauntering about. But my sister threatens to give me further serious trouble, for she has got a most unsuitable marriage in mind. I only hope this bitter cup will pass from me.

Elise had met a sixty-year-old watchmaker, Friedrich Grund – a widower with six children – and Brahms could only shake his head at what seemed to be a general family propensity for wide age differences in their choice of partners. His fears proved to be unnecessary. When Elise did marry her watchmaker she was happier than he had dared hope, greatly comforted in her loneliness by her kind and considerate husband.

Hamburg was still inclined to ignore Brahms the musician. Stockhausen had resigned his post as conductor of the Hamburg Philharmonic the previous year, and Brahms had once more been passed over, despite making his desire for the appointment plain. Extremely bitter though he was, he did not hold anything against Stockhausen and the two set off on a concert tour in March with Brahms's songs as staple fare. After visiting Berlin, Dresden and Kiel, they arrived in Copenhagen. Despite their humiliating defeat in the Prusso-Danish war four years earlier, when Bismarck had annexed the nominally Danish provinces of Schleswig and Holstein, the Danes welcomed the two Germans enthusiastically. After two concerts Niels Gade, who had originally offered support to Brahms's ill-fated manifesto, arranged a reception where they might meet Denmark's leading musicians. The evening went well until Brahms was asked his opinion of the famous Thorwaldsen Museum, and his reply unwittingly turned this piece of small-talk into a political issue: 'It is quite extraordinary. It is only a shame that it does not stand in Berlin.'

Consternation! Not content with Schleswig and Holstein, this Bismarckian wanted to carry off Copenhagen's finest art treasures as well! Everyone present took deep offence, the remark was quoted widely and overnight Brahms found himself completely ostracised. Stockhausen, who had not been so insensitive, could continue the tour through Denmark with Joachim, who arrived just in time, but there was nothing left for Brahms to do but pack his bags in haste and leave for Kiel with his tail very firmly between his legs, his reputation as a tactless boor enhanced by several more degrees.

Yet two weeks later, on 10 April, the Danish incident had been forgotten as Brahms mounted the rostrum to conduct his *Requiem*.

The Leipzig Gewandhaus, where the first performance of the complete German Requiem was given.

Everyone dear to the composer was present: Stockhausen to sing the baritone solo, Brahms's own ladies' quartet to sing in the chorus; in the audience sat Dietrich, the Joachims, Otto Grimm and his wife and, proudest of all, although he did not show it, Jakob Brahms who walked up the cathedral aisle to take his seat with Clara Schumann on his arm. The *Requiem*'s successful combination of tragic loss, radiant consolation and energetic affirmation made a deep impression. Dietrich tells us:

The effect of the splendid performance of this wonderful work was simply overwhelming and it at once became clear to the audience that the *German Requiem* ranked among the loftiest music ever given to the world.

And Clara confided in her diary that evening:

When I saw Johannes standing with the baton in his hand, I could not help thinking of my dear Robert's prophecy: 'When he holds his magic wand over the massed resources of chorus and orchestra, we shall be granted marvellous insights into spiritual secrets,' which is fulfilled today. The baton was a real magic wand that cast its spell on everyone there, even his bitterest foes. It was joy unlike anything I have felt for a long time. After the performance there was supper at the Ratskeller

73

where everyone was overjoyed: it was like a music festival. Reinthaler made a speech about Johannes that moved me so much that (unfortunately!!!) I burst into tears. I thought of Robert and the joy he would have felt if he had lived to see it . . .

Brahms, when asked to make a speech in reply, modestly called three cheers for Reinthaler.

So great was public enthusiasm for the new work that a second performance had to be given in Bremen that same month, though Brahms then returned to Hamburg with the score to write one more section for soprano solo. Although the whole requiem is dedicated to the memory of his mother, this is the section he claimed to be most directly influenced by her. The old lady's memory is movingly enshrined in an autumnal glow of consolation with the words, 'As one whom his mother comforteth, so will I comfort you. Behold with your eyes how that I laboured but a little and found for myself much rest.'

It was almost a year before the *Requiem* was given in its final form at Leipzig. Although it was coolly received there, nothing could stop the work being performed nearly thirty times in different parts of Europe during the next few years. Until he made this work public, Brahms's position as a composer had been an ambiguous one; now, at thirty-five, he justified everyone's belief in him, knowing that his inspiration was based on the firm rock of faultless technique and merciless self-criticism.

The 'young eagle' had spread his wings. Brahms had arrived.

8 Triumph

Flushed with his new-found success, Brahms spent the summer of 1868 in Bonn where he continued to exploit the choral vein. *Rinaldo* was, in Brahms's words, 'carefully polished' and given a new finale, and while staying with the Dietrichs he turned his attention to a text by Hölderlin. Dietrich records: 'Early that morning . . . he had found Hölderlin's poems in the bookcase, and been most deeply moved by the *Song of Destiny*.'

Later in the day they all visited the naval port of Wilhelmshafen.

When . . . after having wandered about and seen everything of interest, we sat down by the sea to rest, we discovered Brahms at a great distance, sitting alone on the beach and writing. These were the first sketches for the *Song of Destiny* which soon appeared.

The poem, comparing the bliss of heavenly spirits with the uncertainty of mortal life, inspired a work of warm, autumnal melancholy from a mind still buzzing with the sounds of the *German Requiem*.

Once more Brahms invited his father to spend the summer with him, and Jakob and he set off down the Rhine as far as Switzerland. Yet Jakob, although revelling in the mountain scenery that contrasted so strongly with the flat landscapes and narrow streets he had known all his life, began to feel his age. Brahms set too fast a walking pace, and at the end of the trip Jakob decided regretfully that he would not undertake such taxing journeys again.

After returning to North Germany with his father in the autumn, Brahms toured the concert circuit of Hamburg, Bremen and Oldenburg and was, as he wrote to Clara, 'plagued with proofs and revisions' of the *Requiem* and the *Magelone* song-cycle. But he yearned for Vienna and was back there in December. Each time he returned to the city his attachment grew stronger and this time, after spending a short period in an hotel, he found temporary lodgings and decided that Vienna would become his base in the future. 'What should I do in Hamburg?' he wrote to his father in April. 'Apart from you there is no one I want to see . . . so I think I shall try to make myself more comfortable in Vienna next autumn.' Restless excursions into the musical world would continue, but with success promising him a more secure existence his focus now shifted firmly from perfidious Hamburg to this

Brahms in his thirties.

alluring musical capital. Walking in the Prater once more, he forgot the chastened melancholy of his choral works and conceived another set of waltzes. In the eighteen *Liebeslieder*, Op.52, for piano duet and vocal quartet, the Viennese waltz lilt is married to texts of love in some of the most engagingly light music Brahms ever wrote. Although he also arranged some for orchestra, with characteristic caution he allowed only the original version to be performed in his lifetime.

March had seen the first performance of *Rinaldo*. He wrote to Simrock:

View near the Prater, Vienna's favourite pleasure garden, where Brahms relaxed in the evenings.

There is, as usual, nothing very brilliant to be said. I don't think I can call it a success. And this time the critical bigwigs listened and really wrote quite a lot . . . everyone expected this time a crescendo of the *Requiem*, and certainly beautiful exciting voluptuous goings-on *à la* Venusberg, on account of Armida, etc.

The Wagnerian theme of knightly temptation and enchantment has been called Brahms's sketchbook for an opera, but he did not regard it as such, being more content with musical representations of key images, such as a magic diamond mirror and a sea voyage, than a stage work with dramatic impetus.

Love, temptation, but certainly not voluptuous goings-on, marred Brahms's summer which was spent once more near Clara at Lichtenthal. He, who had by now stoically resigned himself to bachelorhood, suddenly noticed how beautiful Clara's daughter Julie had become and conceived a deep passion for her. Perhaps he realised the uselessness of his hopes, which were in all likelihood a reflection of his own youthful passion for Clara, for he said nothing. Julie, naturally, saw Brahms simply as the kind honorary uncle who had looked after her as a child; besides, she was in love

A page from the manuscript of the *Alto Rhapsody*, 'the expression of his heart's anguish'.

and already engaged to a young Italian, Count Radicati di Marmorito. When Clara told him of this, however, he was thunderstruck. Clara wrote in her diary at the time:

Johannes is completely different. He rarely comes to the house and when he does, he speaks only in monosyllables. He also treats Julie this way, although he used to be especially kind to her. Did he really love her?

It was a trying enough time for Clara without Brahms's moods. Her son Ludwig was showing the first signs of the mental illness that would confine him to an asylum the following year, and she had only just forgiven Brahms for suggesting the previous year that she give up her 'strolling player' existence on account of her age. It was also the second time that he had created an atmosphere, behaving so rudely to her children the previous year at Lichtenthal that he had almost been banished from Clara's house. On this occasion, Brahms continued to behave badly until September, when Julie was married. Then, on her wedding day, he arrived at Clara's house with a new work which he bitterly called his 'bridal song' and proceeded to play it to her. This was the *Alto Rhapsody*, Op.53, for contralto, male chorus and orchestra, which sets an extract from Goethe's *Winter Journey in the Harz Mountains* depicting a solitary and rejected wanderer in a winter landscape:

Who can comfort his pain if balsam be poison? If he drinks the hatred of men from the fullness of love? The scorned turns to a scorner and devours all his worth alone in arid self-searching.

Clara was deeply touched, writing in her diary that evening:

It is long since I remember being so moved by a depth of pain in words and music . . . This piece seems to me neither more nor less than the expression of his own heart's anguish.

There was undoubtedly a suggestion of self-pity in Brahms's choice of text, but the music is not all arid self-searching, suggesting final consolation in a rapturous sunset glow of choral and orchestral sound. Although he modestly wrote to Dietrich that 'the conductors will not exactly fight for the opus, but it will perhaps be a satisfaction to you to see that I do not *always* write in such a frivolous time as 3/4', he later told him that the music was so dear to him that he slept with a copy of the score underneath his pillow, and would not authorise its first performance until March the following year, when Pauline Viardot sang the solo part at Jena.

Having partly exorcised his emotions, he returned to Vienna and consoled himself with its social round. He was now forming those habits that were to mark his later life with the appearance of routine. Although he still appeared as a virtuoso pianist, and had to undergo the freelance indignities of teaching, and illustrating Hanslick's university lectures with musical examples, he still found time to browse through the bookshops in search of rare manuscripts or to burrow in the archives of the Philharmonic Society whose librarian, Carl Pohl, had now become a close friend. While Brahms was researching there that winter, Pohl showed him the score of a wind partita he had attributed to Haydn with a movement based on an old pilgrim's hymn entitled 'St Antony's Chorale'. Brahms was fascinated by the theme and copied it down for future use.

In the evenings Brahms would often visit friends, or the theatre to see one of Grillparzer's new plays, or he would stroll round the Prater pleasure gardens where he was soon on first-name terms with the ladies of the night. He now toyed with the possibility of a permanent position. Herbeck had left the Philharmonic Society to take up an appointment at the Opera, and Brahms's name was put forward to fill the vacant directorship. Yet once more he was undecided. He was attracted by the possibility of a steady income but feared a loss of freedom. Clara gave her advice:

You have shown often enough how brilliantly you can conduct and no one can approach you in your capacity for grasping things at a glance. In my opinion the only doubtful point is whether you will be able to manage the schoolmaster side of the work, the meticulous practising of pieces; for a true artist this sort of thing is always very trying. Moreover, as a man, it is not your *forte* to be able to communicate your ideas at a moment's notice.

He seemed more interested in writing an opera, telling Clara:

Wagner would not hinder me at all from proceeding with the greatest pleasure to the writing of an opera. Incidentally, in the order of precedence among my wishes, this opera would come before the post of musical director.

Allgeyer had recently furnished him with a libretto, and Brahms now wrote to him:

A man like myself is of very little use in the world. The sort of thing that one could make a decent job of – myself for example, as a conductor and ultimately as the writer of operas and oratorios – doesn't turn up at the right time. Anyhow, do send me the book of *Uthal* . . . I am now pondering over the Jewish liberation from Babylon . . . but I cannot find a satisfactory ending . . . The only thing I can arrive at after much hard thinking is always a 'No'. For instance, *Käthchen von Heilbron* has often attracted me, and now that I have a decent libretto in front of me, all I have learned from it is not to use any text at all . . .

If any text could have set Brahms's operatic juices flowing, Kleist's medieval romantic play should have done, for the author was one of Brahms's favourites. Yet it drew a blank. Clearly, Brahms saw his limitations in this field and decided to pursue the idea of an opera no further in real terms.

While Brahms vacillated over these options others intrigued, and Hellmesberger was appointed to Herbeck's old position. Probably relieved that he had escaped what Levi had called the 'thousand and one petty vexations which are inevitably connected with any official position' in a place like Vienna, where the musical factions were as divided as in any North German town, Brahms left immediately for another summer of wandering. Visiting Munich, he attended a performance of *Das Rheingold*, which he did not like, and the first performance of *Die Walküre*, which he did. He then joined Joachim in Salzburg and was planning to make his usual visit to Lichtenthal when the Franco-Prussian War broke out on 19 July. The trains were stopped and North Germany, as the battle zone, was sealed off. Clara, who was as close to the confused Front as anyone and whose son Ferdinand was called to the colours, wrote from Lichtenthal on 28 July:

Bismarck, architect of German unity. Brahms carried Bismarck's letters in his travelling bag to read wherever he went.

Kaiser Wilhelm I, the focal point of Brahms's patriotism.

Everybody who has a house here . . . is advising me to stay quietly here, for if they can't get enough soldiers billeted on inhabited houses they will open closed ones and use them, and then everything will be ruined . . . If only one knew when the fighting would begin, but everything is so quiet and one hears nothing.

But soon hostilities began in earnest and Brahms was delighted. He saw the French and their scheming, indecisive emperor Napoleon III as the aggressors and later told George Henschel:

So great was my enthusiasm that I was firmly resolved to join . . . the army as a volunteer, fully convinced that I should meet my old father there to fight side by side with me.

Events moved too fast, however, and before Brahms could make up his mind Napoleon had fallen; by September Prussian troops were on their way to Paris. Then, in the *Galerie de Glaces* at Versailles on 18 January 1871, an event occurred that overjoyed the patriotic Brahms: Bismarck engineered the unification of Germany and the Prussian King Wilhelm IV was declared its emperor with the title Kaiser Wilhelm I. 'Long live Bismarck!' Brahms wrote to Levi, and all Brahms's closest friends shared his enthusiasm. Reinthaler had already written to him:

What a time to be alive! My wife says that you must have slipped off to the war, but I think you should save yourself for the world. Dear Brahms, rise up and let God inspire you! Write the *Te Deum* that you must compose.

But Brahms had already done this without any prompting. Spurred on by the earliest Prussian victories at Sedan, he had written the bulk of a vast choral work, the *Triumphlied*, taking his text from the nineteenth chapter of Revelations which seemed to imply that France was the Whore of Babylon that must be overcome. Now, the victorious emergence of the new German state urged him to complete it. He wanted to dedicate it jointly to Bismarck and the new Emperor but, finding that it offended protocol, he dedicated it to the Kaiser alone.

Florence May wrote that Brahms's interest in politics was keen and he seemed to have as intelligent a grasp of the confusing shifts in the political arena as any commentator of his time. His nationalism has embarrassed some, but not those who realise that it was the kind that is bound up with an almost mystical love of the culture and physical appearance of his country, a deep sense of its traditions and a need to bring those traditions to their full flower. Early German Romanticism was deeply involved with this, although it eventually toyed with xenophobic hatred, most especially in Wagner, who was an embryo Nazi before the term was ever conceived, and it reached its most decadent phase in the sinister histrionics of the Third Reich.

Brahms could never be tarred with this vile brush. He would

Brahms, described by Florence May as having 'intense pride . . . intense modesty'.

eventually have seen through such unbalanced thinking, as he saw through Wagner, and would have recognised a lack of that control he exercised so admirably over his own emotions. Bismarck was his politician and Wilhelm his emperor, and through them he saw the emergence of the land he loved from a mess of manipulated provinces to a unity worthy of its greatest men. The *Triumphlied* is jubilant, mainstream Brahms, in the tradition of Handel, not simply an occasional work inspired by passing jingoism. It expresses the triumph of his German pride, although it is also fitting in a personal sense, for Brahms's career was now to consist of a long series of triumphs.

Although the outcome of the war was no longer in question, the newly emerged French Republic maintained a guerrilla campaign that prolonged hostilities. Clara, writing from London where she was once more giving a series of recitals, told Brahms that there was a general air of pro-French sympathy there which she found uncomfortable. The war ended on 10 May with the Treaty of Frankfurt, the new German Empire expanding its borders by taking Alsace and Lorraine from France. Brahms immediately set off for Germany, declaring that he must 'share in the general joy'. He was in Bremen where the first section of the *Triumphlied* was performed under Reinthaler together with the *Requiem* in a benefit concert for the wounded and in memory of the German dead. 'It was overwhelming and grand', Dietrich recalls.

After visiting Berlin, Brahms settled down in Lichtenthal for the rest of the summer. Here he finished the *Song of Destiny* with a consolatory warmth that belies Hölderlin's bleak text. Here also, at Clara's house, he gave lessons to Florence May, who wrote her impressions of the composer as he was in the most confident years of his life:

His most striking physical characteristic was the grand head with its magnificent intellectual forehead, but the blue eyes were also remarkable from their expression of intense mental concentration. This was accentuated by a constant habit he had of thrusting the rather thick under-lip over the upper, and keeping it compressed there, reminding one of the mouth in some of the portraits of Beethoven. His nose was finely-formed. Feet and hands were small, the fingers without 'cushions'.

. . . His dress, though plain, was always perfectly neat in those days. He usually wore a short, loose, black alpaca coat . . . He was near-sighted, and made frequent use of a double eyeglass that he wore hanging on a thin, black cord round his neck. When walking out, it was his custom to go bare-headed and to carry his soft felt hat in his hand, swinging his arm energetically to and fro. The disengaged hand he often left behind him.

In Brahms's demeanour, there was a mixture of sociability and reserve which gave me the impression of his being a kindly-hearted man, but one whom it would be difficult really to know . . . His manner was absolutely simple and unaffected. . . . The intense pride which is equally inherent with intense modesty in the higher order of genius had its share in causing Brahms's reticence about all things concerning himself.

82

In the evenings, she observed, he would walk to Baden-Baden to hear his 'particular friend' Johann Strauss performing the waltzes he so admired, and she gave a first-hand account of his teaching methods, which were almost exclusively based on Bach: only with great reluctance could he be persuaded to play any piece of his own.

After hearing a performance of the *Song of Destiny* at Karlsruhe on 18 October, conducted by Levi, Brahms returned to Vienna. Here, at Christmas, he took the sub-tenancy of two furnished rooms on the third floor of a house, number four, Karlsgasse. It seemed a makeshift arrangement, as his other lodgings in the city had been, but Brahms found that this unprepossessing apartment exactly suited his simple needs: it was quiet and central with a view of the St Charles Church and square where the tiny Wienfluss was spanned by the Elisabeth Bridge, and it was close to the Philharmonic Society building with its concert hall and library. He could not have known it then, but this was to be his base for the rest of his life.

No sooner had he settled in than he received bad news. A letter from his stepmother in January 1872 summoned him to Hamburg, where his father had fallen dangerously ill. When he arrived he found the old man suffering from cancer of the liver. He died shortly afterwards, on 11 February.

Now there was nothing to bind Brahms to Hamburg. His relations with his brother were strained. Fritz, a workmanlike although uninspired musician, had had to bear the stigma of Johannes's fame for years and had even spent the period from 1867 to 1870 in Venezuela to escape jibes of being 'the wrong Brahms'. But he was not altogether guiltless. He always refused to help his family, in spite of having a steady income from teaching, and it was only as they sat beside their dying father that the two brothers called a truce, although they never grew any closer. Elise was happily settled with her husband, so no longer needed his aid.

After Jakob's death, Caroline declared that she would not be a burden to anyone and went back to running a boarding house. Brahms respected her more than either his brother or sister, and regarded her and her children with deep affection, always helping them when he could in later years. In a letter he wrote to her on his return to Vienna, he addressed her as 'mother', and continued:

I know too well what we have lost, and how lonely your life has become. I hope, however, that now you are doubly conscious of the love of others – and, finally, my own love, which is entirely and wholly yours.

The Brahms family had now gone its separate ways. Although Brahms would keep constantly in touch, visit, and help his sister with many gifts of money over the years, he knew that Hamburg could never be his home again. He moved the last of his belongings, including his large collection of books and manuscripts to Karlsgasse 4, and with this final gesture, Vienna captured him entirely.

9 Respectability

As though to set a seal on its newly adopted son, Vienna offered Brahms the directorship of the Philharmonic Society concerts. In doing so it hoped for some measure of stability: both Hellmesberger and his successor Rubinstein had resigned in a flurry of intrigue, and audiences had dwindled as a result. Although he had expressed interest in this post, Brahms was still in mourning and had qualms about public life, as this letter written to Clara at Easter 1872 shows:

I always enjoy festivals in solitude, quite alone, with perhaps just a few dear ones in my room, and very quietly – for are not all my people either dead or far away? . . . For after all I am dependent on the outside world – the hurly-burly in which we live. I do not add my laughter to its medley of voices, nor do I join its chorus of lies – but it is as if the best in man could shut himself up, and only half of him sallied forth dreaming . . .

Yet he hesitated only long enough to extract the best terms from his prospective employers – a handsome salary and complete freedom in artistic matters – before accepting control of the massive choral and orchestral body.

With the prospect of financial security, Brahms spent a carefree holiday in Lichtenthal. In nearby Karlsruhe on 5 June he heard Levi conduct the first performance of the completed *Triumphlied* with its sonorous new closing chorus, which was received with 'wild enthusiasm'. Yet he began to have second thoughts about the work, regarding it as perhaps too unbalanced in its sympathies now that the war with France was receding into memory. He let it be known that he would prefer that there were no more performances, although the ban was not imposed, and the work continued to meet with acclaim throughout Germany.

Almost his first task on taking up the new Viennese appointment that autumn was the methodical sacking of every musician who did not meet his rigorous standards. He then began drilling his choir and orchestra with far more rehearsals than had been the practice to date, although he remembered his problems with the *Singakademie* and was more cautious with programme planning. He introduced many unusual works, nevertheless. Over the three years he held the post, cheek by jowl with tried favourites such as Beethoven's *Missa Solemnis* and works by Berlioz, went Handel's oratorios, Bach's *St Matthew Passion*, and obscure works by Mozart, Mendelssohn and Schumann. Only New German

music was omitted. His love of authenticity in presenting old
music even went as far as the use of a harpsichord, which was a
daring piece of antiquarianism in the days of the piano virtuoso,
although his respect for the music never permitted the dry
intellectual authenticity that has grown up since his death.

Initially, the concerts were fraught with minor disasters, but as
Brahms got into his stride they knitted together and were soon
well-attended and favourably received. His first season was,

however, darkened by news of the death of Julie Schumann in November. She had been in delicate health for some years and had suffered greatly towards the end. Brahms, writing his Christmas and New Year greetings to Clara, must have recalled the brief passion he had nursed for the girl, and after alluding to her loss added:

It is obvious that we who go on living must see many things vanish with the years – things with which it is more difficult to part than with years of life . . . No one can be more attached or devoted to you than I am.

Clara recovered sufficiently to revisit London in February where she sent Brahms news of his increasing fame in England. His first Sextet had been performed 'with very great success', and the second Serenade was also performed at a Crystal Palace concert: 'Joachim tells me it was very well received.'

At the end of the first season Brahms seemed to be irritated by his administrative duties and hinted to Clara that he might give up the post. But when summer arrived he put the cares of his *Conzertwinter* aside and went to relax near Munich in the village of Tutzing on the Starnberger lakeside. He fell in love with the place, writing to Levi:

We have just had a gorgeous thunderstorm, the lake was almost black, but magnificently green along the shores . . . In the background there is a range of snow-covered mountains – one can never see enough of it.

Levi, Luise Dustmann, Allgeyer and other friends visited him from Munich, and Brahms felt very much at home with the simple life of the village, even helping to prepare the vegetables at the local inn where he took his meals. It was a holiday as productive as it was agreeable, for he put the finishing touches to his first string quartet, in C minor, Op.51, and immediately composed a second in A minor, with the same opus number. The granite-like first quartet shows a determination to be at all costs worthy of the sublime Beethoven series, even in its choice of key. The sense of strain induced by this terror of comparison is acute and it is not as grateful on the ear as the second quartet, where he allows his lyrical gift more scope. He also composed his first orchestral work for thirteen years. At first the Variations on a theme by Haydn, Op.56a, based on the St Anthony Chorale he had written down in Vienna three years before, were composed for two pianos, but he immediately orchestrated them. This was later to become one of his most popular works in its orchestral form, and Brahms had both versions published later in the year under the same opus number. Although he often arranged his works for two pianos so that his friends might play them through in private, the only other work he published in both forms was the piano quintet in F minor.

September was marred by a disagreement with Clara and Joachim. They were organising a festival in Bonn to help pay for a

A page from the manuscript of the Haydn Variations.

memorial to Robert Schumann and had earlier asked Brahms whether he would produce a new work for the occasion or prefer his *Requiem* to be performed. Brahms, lax as often, obscure and indecisive in reply, had left the matter open although he tacitly assumed that a performance of the *Requiem* was a foregone conclusion. In the end, no work by Brahms was scheduled for performance and only the intercession of mutual friends smoothed over bad feeling on both sides. At the last minute Brahms swallowed his pride and attended the festival as a tribute to the composer he had most loved and admired.

The quarrel was patched up, and Clara soon sent him her opinion of his two quartets, heard in Munich that November: 'You can imagine with what interest I listened to them and *enjoyed* them.' She had little else to enjoy at the time. Her father had died in October, and the onset of arthritis in her arm had turned a splendid performance of Brahms's piano concerto into a painful ordeal at Leipzig earlier in the year. It was soon to become so unbearable that for long periods she had to dictate her letters, which she loathed. Her son, Felix, too, was suffering from the first stages of tuberculosis. A division between Brahms and herself was unthinkable, despite the occasionally bitter differences of opinion that surfaced between them. His music was her chief consolation: 'I have enjoyed happy – I might say blissful hours, thanks to your concerto,' she wrote, and later, in a letter signed 'Your old Clara':

To witness your growing fame constitutes the happiest experience that the latter years of my life could bring . . . think of the lonely friend who is concentrating all her mind upon you now . . .

For Brahms she was a stable emotional base and mother-substitute to whom he wrote frequently, trying to put her worries into perspective. He no longer wore his heart on his sleeve, as he had in the early days of their relationship; his gestures were more subtle. Thinking of Felix's condition, he set two of his poems to music and sent them unannounced to the family, to their great delight.

During his second season of concerts in Vienna, Brahms conducted the first performance of his Haydn Variations. It was well received, which must have given the cautious composer renewed confidence in the great project that had lain incomplete for almost twenty years, and he now took up the Symphony in C minor with determination.

A new woman friend was about to become Clara's rival for his attentions. In January 1874 he visited Leipzig at the invitation of one of his staunchest admirers, the composer Heinrich von Herzogenberg, who had organised a Brahms festival in the city. The festival was a success and Brahms discovered to his delight that Heinrich was married to a former pupil of his – the mercurial and witty Elisabeth von Stockhausen. Now that this 'slender woman in blue velvet and golden hair', as Brahms called her, was harnessed to the worthy Herzogenberg, Brahms relaxed in her company, and a friendship grew up between the three that was to sustain Brahms for many years. She was to provide his life with new sparkle and the letters she eventually wrote regularly to him were full of shrewd criticism, intelligence and a sense of fun that Clara's increasingly sad epistles could never match.

Brahms, who was so critical of himself, could not abide bad music, and unfortunately Heinrich's fell into this category as far as he was concerned. Time and again Brahms was to avoid commenting on Heinrich's latest scores. He later told a friend: 'there is only one blot on our relationship – if only the man would not compose!' He could see that Heinrich followed the same musical ideals as himself and was often greatly influenced by his compositions, but as he sighed to Clara, 'there is certainly an element of tragedy about becoming in the end too clever for one's needs.'

With two new friends gained, Brahms left for his summer holiday in Switzerland that year. He stayed at Rüschlikon – a lakeside resort near Zurich, famous for its crayfish and fine wines.

Elisabeth von Herzogenberg. Brahms described her as 'this slender woman in blue velvet and golden hair'.

Here he may have continued work on the symphony but otherwise his compositions were all relaxations, intimately written for the voice, including two new sets of songs Op.63 and the *New Liebeslieder*, Op.65, for vocal quartet and piano duet. During a visit to Zurich, where he heard a performance of his *Triumphlied* at a music festival on 11 July, he met the poet J. V. Widmann who was later to write an intimate account of the friendship that grew up between them. They warmed to each other at their first meeting in the house of the composer Hermann Goetz, and Widmann was immediately struck by Brahms's broad view of the events of his times:

How wide was Brahms's intellectual horizon, how clear and healthy his mental vision, and how ripe his judgement of subjects having no immediate connection with his art!

89

They spent the next few days in each other's company, and Widmann was especially impressed by Brahms's love of a good practical joke. One morning a ponderous Swiss musicologist invited himself to their café table and began enthusing about Brahms's music, declaring that he knew every note that he had written. As the eulogy continued, Brahms's face grew more and more serious, for he hated praise. Just then, the band played a march by a minor tunesmith and Brahms silenced his admirer by claiming the work as his own. 'I still seem to see that good man before me as he stood there gaping and listening with upturned eyes to the rather common music,' Widmann smiled, while Brahms whispered 'Well fooled!'

Brahms spent some time with the Widmann family in Berne that summer and, apart from talking about anything and everything with his new friend, he was delighted to discover that Widmann owned one of Beethoven's pianos. Unfortunately it was not in a playable condition, so he had to be content with performing Bach and one or two pieces by himself on the other family instrument. Then, throwing seriousness to the winds, he picked up Widmann's five-year-old daughter, Johanna, who had become very attached to him, and trotted round the streets with her on his shoulders, to the great joy of the little girl and the great astonishment of the good citizens of Berne.

Returning to Vienna for the winter season, Brahms began to

Berne, where Brahms stayed with the Widmanns and trotted around the streets with their little daughter on his shoulder.

90

Beethoven on his deathbed. Brahms was overawed when he visited the room in which Beethoven had died.

find his official appointment intolerable. The administration and in-fighting absorbed as much time as rehearsals, and the recent economic crises of the Austrian government, ending with the crash of the stock exchange, had ruined many concert-goers so attendances were poor. He expended too much energy for too unsatisfying a result and, having proved that he could rise to such a position, he no longer required the status it afforded him in society. Financially he was better off too: Simrock's business acumen had brought him a comfortable income from royalties and would eventually make him a moderately wealthy man. He regarded intrigues to replace him with the popularising Herbeck disdainfully, but bowed to an inner desire for more free time to compose. So, after conducting a triumphant performance of his *Requiem* at the end of the season, which successfully stole the thunder from Wagner who had introduced excerpts from *The Ring* earlier in the week, Brahms resigned and let Herbeck move back.

The Philharmonic Society was sorry to see him leave. It held a ceremony at which he was presented with an illuminated address and bombarded with high-flown verse that bored him almost to the point of rudeness. Then they gave a banquet which he enjoyed much more.

Now, in his early forties, food was becoming one of Brahms's abiding passions and his life was taking on the unalterable rhythm of a bachelor in his middle years. He had received the first of many honours – the Bavarian Order of Maximilian – in the previous year, and was regarded as a composer of the first rank even by those musicians who deplored his classical style. It was time to relax a little. He began to grow a beard to hide his still youthful appearance, but soon shaved it off: the famous full beard was yet to come. He gave up his arduous virtuoso tours, deciding that the only music he would perform in public would be his own. He led a regular life, rising early to devote the morning to composition, the afternoon to strolling round the Prater or browsing in the bookshops, the evening to friends or the theatre, or the famous small restaurants that Vienna had made her own. George Henschel, the *lieder* singer who had sung in Bruch's *Odysseus* at Brahms's final Philharmonic concert, spent a few days relaxing with him afterwards, and records:

Brahms was very fond of sitting with good friends over his beer or wine or his beloved 'kaffee' . . . till the small hours of the day . . . We went for a walk together every day, mostly in the Prater . . . The numerous public gardens where gypsy bands played especially attracted us and it was a delight to notice the increased spirit those brown sons of the Putszta put into their music in the presence of the master who had done so much toward opening up to their beloved tunes a wider sphere of popularity.

Henschel was also present to witness a significant tribute. On 26 March 1875, the forty-eighth anniversary of Beethoven's death,

Brahms had gone with friends to the actual room where he had died. At the exact hour of his passing they all went silent, and when they spoke again, it was in a 'subdued whisper'.

It is possible that in the silence Brahms thought once more of the last challenge that he must meet and overcome, and there could be no more concrete example than this of the unearthly shadow that Beethoven cast over him.

10 Beethoven's Heir

'You don't know how that fellow dogs my footsteps,' Brahms once said of Beethoven, and later, 'There are asses in Vienna who take me for a second Beethoven'.

There is nothing more potent than an idea that takes hold of the public's imagination, and the idea that Brahms was Beethoven, somehow reincarnate, exercised a long fascination over Vienna. The comparison in some ways cried out to be made and was not entirely musical: both were bachelors, both undersized (five foot five inches tall), both carelessly dressed; both famous for their general prickliness when besieged by 'asses' and both rather fond of a drink. When this stocky little composer walked their streets it seemed to the Viennese that Beethoven himself was still among them, and they naturally speculated long and hard about the inevitable symphony that 'Beethoven's heir' must write for them. Clara and Dietrich had seen the first movement of the C minor symphony as early as 1862 and Clara had received the main theme of the finale as a cryptic greeting accompanying a German folk-poem in 1868. Naturally, Brahms's closest friends were intrigued as well, and longed for him to cross the last of Beethoven's barriers.

But the secretive composer shrank back until the last possible moment. Although the final break with the Philharmonic Society had cleared the decks for his masterpiece, he preferred to spend the summer of 1875 in Ziegelhausen, near Heidelberg, working on 'useless trifles to avoid facing the countenance of a symphony', as he wrote to a friend. The 'useless trifles' included his third and last string quartet in B flat major, Op.67 – a much brighter affair than its two predecessors, closer to the spirit of Haydn than to Beethoven – some vocal duets and the Piano Quartet in C minor, Op.60, which, although the first he had begun, was the last he completed. He saw this work as a summing-up of his grand passion for Clara, for it was now twenty years old. Passing it to Simrock, he attached a letter in which he deliberately mocked his own adolescence by recalling the wildly romantic image of Werther:

You could put a portrait on the title-page! A head with a pistol in front of it. That will give you an idea of the music. I'll send you my photograph for the purpose! Can you also have a blue frock-coat, yellow breeches and top-boots as you seem to enjoy colour printing?

93

Beethoven, with whom
Brahms was constantly
compared – and he resented
it: 'There are asses in
Vienna who take me for a
second Beethoven.'

Yet for all the affectionate parody the older and wiser Brahms
bestowed on his younger self, he must have known how closely he
had once steered to that wind.

Ziegelhausen was a great success. Not only was he surrounded
by friends including Anselm Feuerbach, Levi and Dessoff, but by
some of the 'charming lady singers' that always stirred his especial
libido. For relaxation, he immersed himself in books of legends
and fairy-tales and went for long walks beside the River Neckar,
itself a crucible of some of the most potent German legends. He
described himself as 'only too gay' and was well liked by the
populace, especially the children, who followed him about and
rarely left without a present of sweets from his capacious coat
pockets.

But the symphony was never far from his mind. He worked on it
intermittently during the winter, though he interrupted this to
travel to Holland as pianist in his own works. He stayed at
Utrecht, taking up an invitation he had received from Professor
Engelmann and his pianist wife, whom he had first met in Zurich.
They looked after him so well that he dedicated his new string

Utrecht: Brahms regarded
Holland as his second
home.

quartet to the professor as a token of appreciation. Brahms often
returned to Holland, where his music was always warmly and
intelligently received and where he had few problems with the
language, which was so close to his own Hamburg dialect.

An unexpected honour awaited him on his return to Vienna in
April 1876: the University of Cambridge offered him an honorary
doctorate of music. This pleased him greatly until Clara wrote:

I suppose you will have to go there and take your degree in cap and gown.
Joachim was saying only a little while ago that he was going there for that
purpose, so it looks as if you would have to go as well. It is easier to bear
honours than to go there and receive them.

Brahms cooled immediately. He could not be induced in any
circumstances to travel to England. The reasons were nothing to
do with any hatred he might have nursed for that country, which
appreciated his music as much as any other, but with his horror of
sea-travel. Clara had written disagreeable accounts of her channel
journeys: 'The sea was so rough that no ship could cross,' was a
frequent lament. Brahms also considered the English over-formal.
'You have to live in a dress suit there,' he is reported to have
remarked – a situation that would have proved intolerable to the
baggy-suited Brahms. So he wrote asking the university if he
might receive the degree *in absentia*, and let the matter rest.

Sassnitz, on the Baltic island of Rügen, was the nearest Brahms

Rügen, where Brahms
finished his First Symphony
and hopped after frogs.

would go to the sea, and George Henschel had already persuaded him to forego the lakes and rivers of Austria and Germany and join him that summer in the breezy seaside resort. On the way there Brahms called on Clara, who was still living and teaching in Berlin and, as she had already guessed that 'the next thing you will give us will be a symphony', he showed her the score of the nearly completed work.

Once settled on the island, he received a letter from Elisabeth von Herzogenberg, teasing him:

I remember hearing they give you nothing to eat but pale grey beef and indescribable wobbly puddings made of starch and vanilla . . . the person who told me her own bitter experiences was reduced to living on eggs which she boiled or fried in the privacy of her own room.

Brahms did not have to resort to this. He found himself well fed and enjoyed the surroundings. Writing to Clara, he enthused:

Rügen is very, very beautiful apart from the old Low German in which I am at last able to indulge again. There is the most beautiful forest coming right down to the sea here . . . My room is beautifully situated, my window looks out on the sea, the village straggles up the hill to my left and cornfields in front of me are for the present providing the murmuring roll of the waves.

Here he drew the threads of the symphony together, and even Henschel seemed to feel the shadow of Beethoven on him as he did so, writing in his diary at the time: 'His whole appearance vividly recalls some of the portraits of Beethoven.'

96

George Henschel, Brahms's holiday companion.

But it was not all work. A previous experience of sharing a room with Brahms had driven Henschel out into the night, because of the composer's loud snoring, and he now found it advisable to sleep in another hotel, but the two spent most of the day together even so. They swam and dived, wide-eyed, for pebbles, or went for long walks to a heath where Brahms had found a frog pond. He loved to catch the little creatures and set them leaping about, imagining from their pitiful croaking that they had all been transformed from fairy-tale princes and princesses. 'Listen', he commanded, 'there it is again, the poor king's son with his yearning, mournful C flat,' and he incorporated this into several songs he wrote at the time.

Dozing in a hammock overlooking the sea, Brahms talked of his guarded admiration for Wagner: 'I must confess *Walküre* and *Götterdammerung* have a great hold on me. For *Rheingold* and *Siegfried* I do not particularly care.'

Yet when Henschel told him of a death in Wagner's orchestra reported in the newspapers, Brahms replied laconically, 'the first corpse'.

Henschel had to leave Sassnitz to fulfil some concert engagements, and Brahms came down with him to see him off. As the carriage pulled away, all Henschel could see was an image of a titan in Beethoven's mould: 'Nothing but moor, and clouds and – Brahms,' he wrote in awe.

Brahms never returned to Rügen. It had been an interesting departure from the normal round, but for a man grown accustomed to Vienna it was 'too uncomfortable', he decided on reflection. But it had worked its influence on the rugged contours of the symphony, and all that needed to be done to the score was a little tidying up. In August he made a detour to Hamburg to visit his sister and found her tolerably content with her aged husband; he then moved on to Lichtenthal, where Clara was spending the summer as usual, and there he put the finishing touches to his massive score.

While he was there a most tantalising appointment was offered to him: director of music in Düsseldorf – Schumann's old post. Only Schumann's memory could have made him reconsider his decision never again to hold an official appointment, and for this reason he maintained interest in the offer after his return to Vienna in the autumn, asking for details, marshalling support, sounding out Clara. Clara was helpful but unenthusiastic, writing to him in September: 'It will be necessary to have a thick skin and to exercise great authority.'

Düsseldorf had no real attractions any more for Brahms. He had outgrown the town with his youthful enthusiasms and it was too small after cosmopolitan Vienna. Later, he confided to Billroth: 'I can be a bachelor without any further discussion in Vienna, but in a small city, an old bachelor is simply a caricature.'

A much more important event delayed Brahms's decision. Still very wary of his symphony, he arranged for a first performance far

97

The Landestheater,
Karlsruhe, where Brahms's
First Symphony had its
première.

from musical factions and expectations in 'a small town which possessed a good friend, a good conductor and a good orchestra' as he wrote to Dessoff, who immediately offered to conduct the work in Karlsruhe. There, on 4 November, Brahms pinned his symphonic colours to the mast.

'All my thoughts are with you,' Clara wrote to him on the day. 'I hope that you will be quite satisfied.' Brahms was, although the applause was not overwhelming and the praise was faint. Mannheim heard it next and then, on 17 December, Brahms braved comparison in Beethoven's own city.

The Viennese listened to the surging themes and the tense emotional struggles in Beethoven's favourite key of C minor, and noted a similarity between the finale and that of Beethoven's Choral Symphony. 'Any donkey can see that,' Brahms snapped testily. But Hanslick enthused: 'No other composer has come as close to Beethoven's splendid works,' and the symphony was promptly labelled 'Beethoven's Tenth', much to Brahms's chagrin.

In January 1877 Brahms was nervously anticipating a performance he was to conduct in that most fickle of musical centres, Leipzig. Writing to Elisabeth von Herzogenberg from Vienna, he fretted:

Three days before the concert I begin to perspire and drink camomile tea; after the fiasco, attempts at suicide, and so on. You will see the lengths to which an exasperated composer will go!

In the circumstances, suicide was not required: Mendelssohnian Leipzig acclaimed the symphony with loud applause and Brahms enjoyed his stay with the Herzogenbergs, though after he had left Elisabeth opined humorously:

98

I was mad to ask you at all, you spoilt creature, with your mock-turtles, your Prater manners and your constitution ruined by every conceivable refinement of luxury . . .

She, like Clara who was also present at the Leipzig performance, soon hoped to see the published score:

Please have the symphony published soon; for we are all symphony-sick, and weary of straining to grasp the beloved, elusive melodies.

Brahms conducted another performance at Breslau on 23 January which, as he told Clara, was 'very fine'. Although Wagnerian Munich disapproved of the work, as was only to be expected, nothing could stop its triumphant progress.

Finally hearing that Cambridge could not confer a degree *in absentia*, Brahms reluctantly forewent the honour, but in gratitude entrusted a copy of the symphony to Joachim, who was going there to receive his own doctorate. Joachim conducted it on 8 March in Cambridge, assuring Brahms's reputation among discerning English audiences. Later in the year the Philharmonic Society of London awarded Brahms its gold medal which, as it did not require a personal attendance, he gladly accepted.

Now that the long battle with Beethoven was nearly won, Brahms could relax in the full knowledge of his powers. His innately bourgeois craving for the respectability of a label no longer required a titled position to justify itself. Düsseldorf's meagre attractions receded and, prompted by Clara's bitter reflections on the post: 'You can do better than go there to wage a perpetual battle with vulgarity which is always in the majority in Düsseldorf where right-minded people are few and far between,' he rejected this attempt to capture him as a debt of honour to Schumann's memory. The symphony had justified him. From henceforth, the label of 'composer' was sufficient for Brahms.

11 Intermezzo

Brahms had laboured and agonised over his First Symphony for twenty years, but the creative flood-gates now opened. During the next decade Brahms was to turn more to the orchestra, composing those symphonies and concertos that have since made his name a household word.

In June 1877 he left Vienna for his summer holiday. He chose an unspoiled village, Pörtschach on the Wörthersee in southern Austria, and from the first moment felt at his ease with the unpretentious sort of people he always preferred, striking up friendships with the comfortable Kupelweiser family from Vienna and the local doctor, among others. He enjoyed meeting them at Werzer's hotel, where he would take his coffee and read his newspaper overlooking the lake and surrounding mountains. His host's daughter, Christine Werzer, helped him pack his manuscripts for Simrock. He became very friendly with his 'little postmistress' as he called her, and she in her turn considered the prickly, middle-aged composer 'charming'. He probably was charming, for he was in the best of moods: 'So many melodies fly about that one must be careful not to tread on them,' he remarked, and in a letter to Clara he says:

I have just been on a walking tour for two days in the Ampezzo valley . . . You would be enchanted . . . above all with the mountains (the Dolomites with all their strange shapes and shades which one never grows tired of looking at), the lakes, the flowers, the magnificent highways and everything.

This rapturous sense of well-being found its way into a second symphony, in D major, Op.73, which he now composed with amazing rapidity. He was so effortlessly inspired that, when he moved to Lichtenthal at the end of August, the work was nearly complete; it had taken him a mere three months and he had also found time to compose his first motet and some songs. He finished the symphony at Lichtental then took time off in September, going to Mannheim to attend the first performance of Goetz's opera *Francesca da Rimini*. Goetz had died the previous year at the age of thirty-five and this pilgrimage, by way of posthumous tribute to a friend Brahms had never really admired as a composer, is typical of the curious loyalty of the man. At the performance he met Widmann again and the operatic circumstances seemed to revive Brahms's interest in

Pörtschach, where Brahms wrote his Second Symphony, described by Billroth as 'All rippling streams, blue sky, sunshine and cool green shadows'.

writing an opera of his own. Widmann discussed the matter with him exhaustively. He knew that Brahms had 'extraordinary dramatic instinct', as his comments on plays they had visited together seemed to show, but found that he was held back chiefly by the foolishness of most libretti and a distaste for drama set entirely to music. But he did suggest that Widmann, who had already written a successful libretto for Goetz's popular *Taming of the Shrew*, might cobble one together for him. He had several suggestions, but seemed to be especially drawn to Gozzi's dramatic fable *König Hirsch*, which contained such curiosities as a magician who transforms a king into a stag.

Leaving Widmann to mull over his idea with some perplexity (he secretly considered the play to be a 'grotesque and extravagant farce' – was this another of Brahms's jokes?), Brahms returned to Vienna. Here he was offered and accepted the only type of official position that he found congenial. Herbeck had died in October, leaving his post as commissioner to the Austrian Ministry of Education vacant, and Brahms was happy to accept his chair in an advisory capacity, thus allowing him to recommend grants to struggling young composers.

Rehearsals of the new symphony now began. His closest friends had not seen it, and were intrigued, so Brahms kept up a playful correspondence with Elisabeth over the true nature of this genial work, writing to her in November:

101

I shall not need to play it to you beforehand. You have only to sit down at the piano, put your small feet on the two pedals in turn and strike the chord of F minor several times in succession, first in the treble, then in the bass (*ff* and *pp*), and you will gradually gain a vivid impression of my 'latest'.

And on 29 December, the day before its first performance under Hans Richter at the Philharmonic Society, in a letter signed 'Ever your unwashed J. Br.', he told her:

The orchestra here play my new symphony with crêpe bands on their sleeves because of its dirge-like effect. It is to be printed with a black edge too!

But of course Brahms's sunny symphony was received with smiles and enthusiastic applause, especially the third movement, which had to be repeated. When the applause finally ceased, one member of the audience remarked loudly, 'Never forget that you have had the pleasure of listening to this music,' and Billroth had already given his opinion:

It is all rippling streams, blue sky, sunshine and cool green shadows. How beautiful it must be at Pörtschach!

The Viennese agreed and, enamoured now of the Beethoven comparison, immediately dubbed it 'Brahms's Pastoral Symphony', evoking more remarks about 'asses' from the composer's sarcastic lips.

Simrock published the two symphonies together at the end of the year, while Brahms went on to Leipzig to conduct the Second Symphony. He stayed at the Herzogenbergs', having playfully taken the precaution of commanding Elisabeth 'not to burn the food' this time. The symphony was rather coldly received, possibly because Leipzig felt duty bound to disagree with Vienna in the best traditions of musical in-fighting. Brahms was not discouraged, and travelled next to Hamburg where he conducted his First Symphony, but lingered only long enough to glance dismally at his former home town and write to Elisabeth:

The weather is vile as only Hamburg weather can be – and is, on 360 days in the year. (It is difficult enough to hit the other five.) Not an hour, the whole time, when you feel inclined to go out, or even look out of the window.

But the weather did not spoil his tour. He seemed to enjoy presenting his two symphonies in sequence: Bremen heard the Second on 22 January 1878, Utrecht heard the First a few days later. He stayed with his old friends, the Engelmanns, who looked after him with their usual care. He wrote an account to Clara:

In Utrecht it was . . . very pleasant – wreaths, an honorary membership . . . A small choir sang my love songs in quite exemplary fashion and repeated them two days later.

102

Amsterdam, where Brahms and his music were greeted with enormous enthusiasm.

He was in Amsterdam next, which proved a cheerful contrast to the gloom of Hamburg. Here he performed the Second Symphony twice, such was the overwhelming public enthusiasm for the work, then it was the turn of The Hague. 'Holland is really charming,' he wrote to Elisabeth. 'I lose my head over it each time. Number two takes so well with both musicians and public that it is not spoiling my stay.' This prompted a typically pithy response from Elisabeth: 'We had heard from the Engelmanns how you were being spoiled in Holland.'

After this whirlwind symphonic tour Brahms returned to Vienna, but the new symphony continued its rounds without him, not always triumphantly, as Elisabeth, who attended a performance in Dresden remarked:

The high priest of Dresden critics . . . inquires why you don't confine yourself to chamber music, in which you have done some really good work . . . Who are these people, I should like to know?

We can imagine that Brahms echoed her indignant question, and no doubt had his own unprintable reply.

That March, sitting in his new capacity as Grants Commissioner, Brahms received a composition from Antonin Dvořák, then thirty-six, but completely unknown outside his native Bohemia. He was so impressed that he immediately granted

103

Antonin Dvořák, of whom Brahms said: 'I am beside myself with envy at the ideas that come quite naturally to the chap.'

Rome, visited at breakneck railway speed.

him a scholarship, gave him covert financial assistance and later introduced him to Simrock, who published some of his scores.

'Your warm encouragement and the pleasure you seem to find in my work have moved me deeply and made me unspeakably happy,' Dvořák wrote to Brahms in reply, and Brahms confessed later: 'I am beside myself with envy at the ideas that come quite naturally to the chap.' This kindness paved the way to a friendship that was to last until Brahms's death.

Another foreign tour was planned for April, but this time purely for pleasure. The Herzogenbergs received this letter in Brahms's jauntiest vein:

The undersigned begs to inform his esteemed patrons that letters addressed *poste restante*, Naples, will find him from 14 April to 20th. From the 20th onwards – Rome. He travels with Billroth, and requests orders for writing letters, amputating legs or anything in the world.

On this first Italian tour the two friends were joined by Carl Goldmark, composer of a popular violin concerto and the once highly acclaimed *Rustic Wedding* Symphony, whom Brahms considered 'an excellent fellow'. It was led at breakneck railway speed by the efficient Billroth. Goldmark left them at Rome to attend a performance of his opera *The Queen of Sheba* but Brahms was whisked off to Naples from where Billroth wrote home: 'Brahms is full of warm sensitivity for everything beautiful, and in good spirits. We go almost everywhere on foot.' But in a letter to his friend Ernst Frank, Brahms opined: 'I should be quite content

to have seen Rome. On the way back we shall see it, and anything else that turns up, with thorough desultoriness.'

Florence and Venice were glimpsed on the return in May, but this swift tour, far from turning the sedate Brahms against Italy, merely whetted his appetite. He was dazzled, and visited the country many times in the following years. Widmann, who accompanied him on later journeys, tells of his deep attachment. He loved the passionate yet controlled emotionalism of the people, which he compared unfavourably with the cold reserve and *parvenu* boorishness of the Germans and Swiss. He even refused to believe in the brigands that swarmed all over the ungovernable south. Everything was a delight, from the landscape and High Renaissance art and architecture which he would always 'feel' instinctively, rather than study in a guide-book, down to the food and wine, the painted ceilings and carts, and the 'splendour of the table appointments'. Only Italian music failed to interest him, although he admired Verdi, then at the height of his fame, whom he liked to compare with himself as a 'man of the people'. Even so, he could not be induced to hear any of his operas. Performances went on until after midnight and Brahms never varied his routine of rising at five in the morning, even on holiday.

After Billroth's introduction, however, Brahms felt the need to relax. As the train taking him to Vienna passed the Wörthersee, he decided to stop for a day at Pörtschach to regain his equilibrium. There he remained, writing to Arthur Faber:

The first day was so delightful that I had to stay one more. But the second day was so delightful that I have settled down altogether for the present.

Once in Pörtschach, he cancelled an intended visit to the Lower Rhine Festival in Düsseldorf, where he had been booked to conduct the Second Symphony. The curious reason he gave was that he had no good clothes to wear. Once more, he made his excuses to the Fabers: 'It means a dress-coat and *décolleté*. I must think it over.'

Although his sense of dress was now veering from the comfortable to the positively shabby – an old brown overcoat that his friends tried unsuccessfully to replace is the recurring butt of many a joke in Elisabeth's letters – and he had sprouted a beard in Italy, prompted, perhaps, by the presence of Billroth's luxuriant growth, these matters of appearance were not the real reason. He simply had more important work to do. Italy and Pörtschach had released the lyrical mood once again and he was composing with the same fluency that had produced the Second Symphony the year before. He worked on a series of piano pieces – his first for sixteen years – which he collected as *capricii* and *intermezzi*, Op.76, but his main concern was the violin concerto that he had long promised Joachim. It shared the same mood and key as the symphony and was originally planned on symphonic lines, with four movements in place of the more usual three.

105

As Brahms did not play the violin, he consulted Joachim on various technical points as he composed, although the stubborn composer ignored his friend's advice when he felt the great violinist was going too far. The finale was planned as a Hungarian gypsy rondo. This was a neat compliment to Joachim, who not only was Hungarian but had also written a 'Hungarian' violin concerto himself. When Brahms heard this in 1860 he had been deeply impressed, writing to Clara that it was 'full of restrained beauty and so calm, so deep and warm in feeling that it is a joy'.

This seems as much a description of Brahms's concerto as of Joachim's and it is clear that Brahms hoped to emulate that mood. As if the concerto were not a large enough task, he also began sketching a violin sonata in G, Op.78, which he completed the following year, and probably began collecting ideas for what would eventually be a second piano concerto.

The bearded Brahms had great fun on his return to Vienna – hiding from autograph hunters, visiting friends and colleagues under pseudonyms and generally passing himself off as someone else; but his light-hearted sense of fun was jolted by another ironic communication from Hamburg. The Hamburg Philharmonic Society, who had continually overlooked him, now invited him to conduct his Second Symphony at their fiftieth anniversary celebrations. Brahms, growing more irascible and unforgiving, nursing old wounds, refused immediately, only to relent and arrive in Hamburg to take over the baton at the last moment.

He found the orchestra led by Joachim and filled with old friends, and his dramatic appearance, now publicly bearded for the first time, was greeted with applause that grew more ecstatic as each movement died away. At the end he was recalled many times, and roses fell on him from all sides. Brahms was gratified, but not won over. He did not stay long and soon moved on to Leipzig with Joachim to work on the Violin Concerto.

A 'consultation at the piano' produced the final version. He had already excised the two middle movements, 'they were the best, of course', he joked, and replaced them with a 'feeble adagio' (despite his false modesty, considered the serene emotional heart of the work); then, off the cuff, he decided 'we might as well give them the pleasure at Leipzig', and a first performance of the concerto was scheduled there for 1 January 1879, with Joachim as soloist.

After spending Christmas in Vienna and briefly visiting Berlin, Brahms returned to Leipzig for the concert. But the concerto was not a total success. Several factors worked against it: like the only other Brahms concerto to date, it was symphonic and did not sparkle with the empty virtuoso pyrotechnics of a Paganini or Sarasate. In addition, Joachim was unwell and gave a less than sparkling performance; but Brahms's unconventional dress dealt it the final blow. As he conducted, his trousers, which he had tied up with an old necktie in haste, began to work loose and a larger space was revealed between his shirt and waist as each movement

106

progressed. The staid Leipzigers hoped with horror that the concerto would end before the great composer's trousers fell to his ankles and they naturally did not concentrate as fully on the musical argument as they might have done under normal circumstances. Fortunately, the farcical did not occur, but the applause, if tinged with relief, was distinctly lukewarm.

The Viennese performance on 14 January was not marred by such banalities, and Hanslick recognised the concerto as, 'probably the most important since Beethoven and Mendelssohn'. But Brahms wrote to Elisabeth that it was:

A real down-hill affair after Leipzig; no more pleasure in it. In some trifling ways it was even more successful; the audiences were kinder and more alive. Joachim played my piece more beautifully with every rehearsal, too, and the cadenza went so magnificently at our concert here that the people clapped right on into my coda.

Joachim left for another English tour after this. He played the concerto at a Crystal Palace concert and it was here that it received its first unqualified success. So enthusiastic were the English that Joachim had to repeat the work several days later. On his return, Brahms rejoined him and they introduced the concerto to Bremen, Hamburg and Berlin.

Clara had moved to Frankfurt the previous year to take up a teaching appointment in the Conservatoire, and from there she wrote to Brahms with the sad news that her gifted son Felix, his own god child, had died on 16 February from tuberculosis. Brahms, much affected by this, replied from Berlin:

All the memories of the good things I have had in the past and the thoughts of all the good things I may yet hope for and expect, crowded in upon my mind. At the moment I only feel with double force what I felt before.

It is a good thing that Fate cannot assail me many more times. I very much fear that I should not bear it very well. But what I wish with all my heart is that everything that is given to Mankind and which reaches them from outside, in order to comfort them in their trouble and to help them to bear it, may be vouchsafed to you in abundance.

On his return to Vienna, he found two offers awaiting him. Breslau University wanted to award him an honorary doctorate of philosophy, and Leipzig wanted him to take up Bach's old post of cantor at St Thomas's church. This was another of those tantalising offers that Brahms could never refuse outright, and he considered it quite seriously, especially as the Herzogenbergs lived in the town. Eventually, however, he could not divest himself of his hard-won 'freedom', and declined. The doctorate he accepted in a brief note scribbled on a postcard, and then assumed that, as in the case of Cambridge, nothing else would be required of him. He was soon informed, however, that he would be expected to provide a new symphony, or at least some kind of sung tribute, for the occasion. He put the commission aside for the time being.

He remained longer than usual in Vienna that spring, because of bad weather and a wish to see the silver wedding celebrations of the Austrian emperor and empress. He described these in a letter to Elisabeth as 'beautiful beyond expectation and beyond description'. When he did leave, it was to visit Pörtschach once more. There, as before, he rented his 'seven beds' as he called the large house he took only to leave most of it locked up for privacy. Here he returned to the violin sonata he had begun the previous year, completing its delicate 'raindrop' finale with a direct quotation from his earlier song *Regenlied*. He sent it immediately to Clara who wrote back: 'I had to cry my heart out afterwards for joy over it.' He also completed his Two Rhapsodies, Op.79, for piano. Sending them to Billroth for appraisal, he dismissed them as 'worthless trash', although Billroth thought they harked back to the 'young, heaven-storming Johannes', and Elisabeth, when she saw them at the end of the year, wrote to Brahms: 'You rejoiced my heart by sending those glorious pieces . . . it is hard to believe that there was ever a time when I did not know them.'

In Pörtschach that summer he met Marie Soldat, a nineteen-year-old violinist whose remarkable talent Brahms admired so completely that he appeared with her in a concert given in the village, contrary to his usual rule that he did not perform in the summer. He introduced her to Joachim and spent the rest of the season coaching her in his Violin Concerto, which she later played to great effect in Vienna. The two continued their friendship in the city and would often be seen together in the Prater funfair or at the theatre, and there is no doubt that 'my little soldier', as Brahms nicknamed her, was a great comfort to the increasingly lonely man.

Leaving Pörtschach, Brahms visited Joachim who was staying near Salzburg. The Herzogenbergs were also staying there and the new violin sonata was tried through at their house. For Elisabeth, it was easy to 'lose yourself in blissful dreaming as you listen to it'; but Brahms would have none of this: 'We were none of us quite satisfied with it,' he wrote in reply, and he revised it before he and Joachim included it in the repertory of a concert tour they were planning through Hungary and Transylvania.

Brahms had not toured with Joachim for twelve years and, although they had maintained a close professional relationship, their early friendship had cooled noticeably. Joachim had had his doubts about Brahms as early as 1856, when he had written to Gisela von Arnim:

Brahms has a dual personality: one is mostly naive genius . . . the other is one of devilish cunning which, with a frosty surface, suddenly explodes in a pedantic, prosaic need to dominate.

And Brahms had his reservations about Joachim, being especially annoyed that he had given up the career of a promising composer to become what he saw as a money-spinning virtuoso.

Brahms at the piano – a sketch by Willy von Beckerath. Brahms was reputed to smoke a box of cigars a day.

Now that he had grown older, Brahms feared the discomfort of whistle-stops and one-night musical stands with him, writing to Clara:

I should often feel inclined to undertake these concert tours if one could give a concert every other day and have time to get to know the country and people. But the modern virtuoso is too grasping for this. There has to be a concert every day, and all one can do is to arrive an hour before the concert and be off an hour after it. I can think of nothing more detestable or more contemptible than this kind of occupation.

Despite these qualms, he had to admit on his return that they had had 'a beautiful and most enjoyable journey'. Joachim and he got on so well that they planned a tour of Poland for February 1880, which proved equally successful.

From February to May 1880 Brahms was busy touring the Rhineland towns, staying with old friends such as Willy von Beckerath who was responsible for several whimsical sketches and silhouettes of Brahms. Here he was fêted like a cult figure. In May

Brahms as conductor –
sketches by Willy von
Beckerath.

he was present at the dedication of a monument to Robert
Schumann in Bonn, and a Schumann mini-festival was held there
from 2 to 4 May during which Brahms conducted the stirring
Rhenish Symphony and the *Requiem für Mignon*, Joachim
appearing in a performance of Brahms's Violin Concerto, which
the composer also conducted.

This emotional tribute to the man they had both loved and
admired was the last time that Joachim and Brahms would
collaborate with anything like the old accustomed ease; though
neither could foresee the dramatic events that would break their
friendship apart in little less than a year.

12 Maturity

After the strenuous *Conzertwinter* of 1879–80 Brahms needed his holiday more than usual. But Pörtschach had dropped in his estimation, having turned commercial, and the presence of autograph hunters on the lookout for a great composer was more than tiresome to a man not blessed with much patience at the best of times. He once told Widmann of the lengths these adulate hordes went to in order to get his autograph, sending him letters in which they demanded payment for 'ten dozen rapiers' or, in the case of one Cape Town lady, ordering 'one of his far-famed Viennese pianofortes', in the hope that he would reply with a signed refusal. Of course, he never did.

His choice of Ischl, the society spa near Salzburg patronised by royalty, would, however, seem an odd choice for one seeking peace and simplicity. Elisabeth wrote in amazement: 'What can take you to Ischl? . . I thought half Vienna disported itself there.'

This drew the testy response: 'The whole of Vienna is better than half Leipzig or half Berlin,' and it seemed to be precisely what Brahms wanted, for he was at least able to choose his companions more carefully. Hanslick often visited the resort and Johann Strauss had a country retreat there. Brahms wasted no time in renewing the friendship he had formed at Baden with the master of light music, and soon became a frequent guest at the parties Strauss and his vivacious family threw regularly during the summer months. Here he could enjoy at first hand the waltzes he had tried to emulate, and when Strauss eventually dedicated one to him with 'respect and admiration', he was delighted.

In these civilised surroundings, he turned his thoughts to a work for the forthcoming presentation of his degree at Breslau University. Recalling the student drinking songs he had sung with friends in Göttingen, he collected a few and wrote the *Academic Festival Overture*, Op.80, based on these, rather than the weighty opus considered more appropriate for such an event. But, as always with Brahms, bubbling high spirits had to have their counterpart, so he worked up some old sketches into the turbulent *Tragic Overture*, Op.81. Although breathing the same air as the romantic 'Faustian' overtures popular among the New German composers, it is as rigorously logical as any of Brahms's symphonic movements. Brahms adhered closely to his belief that abstract music refines inner emotion and he gave no clue to the nature of its personal tragedy, if any existed. 'One laughs, the other weeps', is all he would say of the only overtures he ever released.

He also occupied himself with chamber music, composing the bulk of his second piano trio in C major, Op.87, and a work designed specifically for serious students of the piano, uncompromisingly called *51 Didactic Exercises for the Pianoforte*. He would have liked to write another choral work, but could find nothing that cried out for setting, complaining to Elisabeth:

They are not heathenish enough for me in the Bible. I have bought the Koran but can find nothing there either.

Despite the relaxations of parties and waltzes, the summer was marred in several ways. The weather in July was extremely wet and affected Brahms's ears alarmingly. Imagining that the Beethoven comparison had now reached the stage of incipient deafness, he left immediately to consult Billroth in Vienna. Billroth was able to put his mind at rest, however. It was an aural catarrh, and the deafness only temporary; but newspapers had seized the story and, when Brahms returned to Ischl, he received numerous letters of concern from well-wishers that he found tiresome to answer. To Elisabeth, he complained:

I cannot even claim indulgence on account of my distinguished complaint, which proved to be none at all.

112

In this batch of unwelcome letters there was one from Joachim on a different matter that troubled him more deeply. One of the reasons Brahms had found his friend's company irritating in recent years was the almost pathological jealousy he had shown with regard to his wife. Now he openly accused her of being unfaithful with Brahms's own publisher, Simrock. Brahms considered this preposterous, and decided to take Amalie's side. He arranged a meeting with Joachim in Berchtesgaden for September where he tried to persuade him that his suspicions were groundless. He seemed to succeed and the rest of the visit was spent in more relaxed mood at Clara's new holiday home in nearby Vordereck. Here they tried out Brahms's overtures and two movements of his piano trio in one of his arrangements for two pianos, all to general approval.

Thinking he had poured oil on the troubled matrimonial waters, Brahms returned to Vienna in November. There he wrote to Clara:

Heaps of concerts are being given here and my music, particularly the chamber music, is having a terrific vogue.

He amused himself by adapting some of Handel's chamber music for modern instruments; then, after hearing his *Tragic Overture* performed on 20 December, he travelled to Berlin to hear Joachim conduct the *Requiem*. While there, he was distressed to find that his diplomacy of the summer had made little impression on Joachim, who was still at loggerheads with his wife. He returned to Vienna as soon as possible, and wrote a long and intimate letter to Amalie:

I have known of your difficulties as long as they have existed: therefore, let me tell you, first of all, that I have never by thought or word adopted your husband's view, for there never was any reason to do so. I have always – and often – thought of you with sympathy, but now, since I have been with you, how completely I agree with you, how I wish I could do something! . . .

You may, however, have noticed that, in spite of our friendship of thirty years' standing, in spite of all my love and admiration for Joachim, in spite of all the mutual artistic interests which should bind me to him, I am always very careful in my intercourse with him, so that I rarely associate with him for long or at all intimately, and I have never even thought of living in the same town and tying myself down to work with him. Now I hardly need tell you that I knew, even before you did, of the unhappy peculiarity with which Joachim torments himself and others in such an inexcusable way. Friendship and love I must be able to breathe as simply and freely as air. I take alarm when I encounter these beautiful emotions in a complicated and artificial form, and the more so if it has to be maintained and enhanced by painfully morbid excitement.

Needless scenes, evoked by imaginary causes, horrify me. Even in friendship, a partial separation is sad, but it is possible. Thus I have saved a small part of my friendship with Joachim by my caution; without this, I should have lost all long ago . . .

113

I therefore simply want to tell you, explicitly and plainly, as I have told Joachim innumerable times, that it is my opinion and belief that he has done you a grievous wrong; and I can but hope that he will abandon his false and terrible delusions.

This letter, reproduced at length for the light it throws on a normally reticent Brahms as much as on Joachim, caused considerable acrimony when Joachim sued for divorce later in the year. Amalie presented it in court as evidence of her good character and tipped the legal balance in her favour. Joachim considered himself betrayed by one of his oldest friends and from that moment refused to have anything more to do with Brahms the man, although he was too generous an artist to sever connections with his music, which he continued to perform as frequently as before.

These events were still simmering below the surface on 4 January 1881 when Brahms arrived in Breslau for his investiture as Doctor of Philosophy. After the ceremony, he conducted his Second Symphony and the two new overtures. The *Academic Festival Overture* fooled everyone with its solemn introduction, but when the familiar tunes blared out in full symphonic dress, the students were so delighted, according to one report, that they joined in with their own irreverent words, which must have completely satisfied Brahms's sense of mischief.

After paying a fleeting visit to the Herzogenbergs in Leipzig, the new doctor continued his concert tour round North Germany, reaching Holland in February. He then travelled south to Budapest where he met Liszt again. The seventy-year-old Hungarian greeted him cordially, but restraint was necessarily the keynote to their reunion, given the distance each had moved musically from the other.

The recent death of Brahms's friend Feuerbach had moved him deeply, and on his return to Vienna he began work on a choral threnody, *Nänie*, Op.82 to words by Schiller: 'Even the beautiful must die, but it is glorious to be a song of lament in the mouth of a friend.' He also attempted to learn a little Italian, preparing for a second visit to Italy with Billroth that spring.

Before setting off, Brahms cemented a new friendship that was to have beneficial results for his music. Although he had known Hans von Bülow since the early days of his career when the great pianist had championed his first piano sonata, von Bülow's total identification with the Wagner cause had prevented any real further contact. Now, von Bülow had lost his wife Cosima to the insatiable Wagner and the wronged husband took the only revenge available to him: he transferred his covert admiration for Brahms into a full-blooded allegiance, declaring, among other things, that there were only three 'Bs' in music – Bach, Beethoven and Brahms. In addition to being a bellicose propagandist, he was also a painstaking conductor who had recently taken charge of the Duke of Meiningen's orchestra and was transforming it into a

Hans von Bülow, the 'battling baron'.

precision tool. He now took the opportunity of a season of concerts he was presenting in Vienna to contact Brahms directly and put his new orchestra at his disposal. Brahms stored the information away for closer future use than von Bülow had anticipated, then set off for Italy in April.

Nottebohm accompanied Billroth and Brahms and the tour was taken at a more leisurely pace than the first. The train deposited the eager tourists at Venice, Florence and then Siena where Brahms wrote to Clara:

If only you stood for only one hour in front of the façade of the cathedral . . . you would be beside yourself with joy and agree that this alone made the journey worthwhile.

Orvieto and Rome followed, and Brahms wrote again:

On the following day in Orvieto you would be forced to acknowledge that the cathedral was even more beautiful and after all this, to plunge into Rome is an indescribable joy.

From Rome, where Nottebohm left them, they continued to Naples and Sicily which Brahms called 'indescribably beautiful'. Billroth wrote to Hanslick from there:

Five hundred feet above the murmuring waves! Full moon! Intoxicating scent of orange blossoms, red cactus blooming as luxuriantly on the huge, picturesque rocks as moss does with us! Forests of palms and lemons, Moorish castles, well-preserved Greek theatre! The broad line of snow-clad Etna, the pillar of fire! Add to this a wine called Monte Venene! Above all, *Johannes in ecstasy!*

Billroth enlivened the steamer trip back from Sicily by delivering a baby, then, at Rome, he left Brahms to return to Vienna 'in time for the spring'. Brahms lingered a few days in Rome, but was back in Vienna for his forty-eighth birthday and his usual greeting from Clara:

I hope that you will celebrate your birthday wisely but not too well and that the thought of the warm hearts that beat for you in cold Germany will bring a glow to your own.

Brahms did not move far from Vienna that summer, taking a villa at Pressbaum, in the Vienna woods. 'My little villa is quite charming,' he wrote to the Herzogenbergs. There he took up the sketches he had made for his Second Piano Concerto – in B flat major, Op.83. It grew into a monumental and difficult work, a tribute to intellect and virtuosity, incorporating the scherzo originally designed for the Violin Concerto as a fourth movement. He was well pleased with it and in the best of spirits: 'I don't mind telling you that I have written a tiny, tiny piano concerto with a tiny whisp of a scherzo,' he wrote to Elisabeth on completing the score in July. He played the same joke on Clara. Neither was deceived, Elisabeth replying that she was delighted to hear of the 'tiny, tiny *Konzerterl* with a tiny, tiny *Scherzerl*', and Clara, more ponderously, 'I am suspicious of the word "small" . . . I shall be quite satisfied if, after all, I can manage to play it!'

Billroth received the two-piano reduction of the score in July: 'I am sending you some small piano pieces,' Brahms joked once more.

Widmann, who visited Pressbaum in August, wrote a cameo sketch of Brahms relaxing after completing the concerto:

As I walked through the little garden I caught sight of the great musician reading at an open window . . . The sight of his fine flowing beard (which I then saw for the first time, hardly recognising its owner) seemed to me a symbol of the perfect maturity of his powers, and of the knowledge of himself and his aims to which [he] had attained.

When Widmann expressed surprise at the beard, Brahms made his famous reply: 'A clean-shaven man is taken for an actor or a priest.' Widmann mused, 'He had a certain naive pleasure in his personal appearance, and smilingly informed me that his photograph with the beard had been used in a school-book as an illustration of the Caucasian type [Baenitz, *Classbook of Geography – First Course*].'

116

The beard, which he had tried for so long to cultivate in order to overcome the air of inexperience his youthful face presented to the world, had indeed grown long. Hanslick had remarked on it the year before: 'None of Mme Schumann's children is as young as she is. Brahms is cultivating a patriarchal beard with the hope of passing for her father,' and it might have given him one further advantage – Beethoven had had no beard.

On Brahms's return to Vienna that autumn, he and Ignaz Brüll played the 'long terror' – as he now liked to style the concerto – to 'the victims Billroth and Hanslick'. The ordeal was a pleasant one, and both were deeply impressed. Billroth, discerning the influence of Sicily in the music, called its romantic slow movement 'a full moon night in Taormina'. The Herzogenbergs, who were passing through Vienna at the time, also heard the work together with *Nanie* which he had completed at Pressbaum, and were, as usual, delighted.

Armed with praise from the only critics he respected, Brahms decided to take up von Bülow's offer and try the concerto at Meiningen. Arriving there in October, he found conditions ideal. He was soon as much at home with the court as with its orchestra, for Duke George II and his Duchess, a former actress, were far from being the sort of hidebound aristocrats who had made Detmold such an uncomfortable experience. They treated him with sympathy and kindness and he eventually numbered them among his closest friends. The friendship was to deepen over the years. Brahms was presented with Meiningen's finest honours and he was a frequent guest at their hunting lodge on the Königsee or their villa at Lake Como in Italy, as well as Meiningen where he particularly enjoyed the art treasures, music-making and fine theatre. The increasingly shabby composer would actually go out of his way to dress for dinner, wearing all his decorations. His favourite dishes would be presented at table on plates of gold, and he especially loved a silver dinner-bell that had been presented to Mary Queen of Scots by Cardinal de Guise.

Meiningen, an aristocratic haven.

117

The concerto went into rehearsal at Meiningen but Brahms reserved the first performance for Budapest. He played the taxing piano part himself there on 9 November, to respectful applause, then returned to Meiningen to perform it on 27 November. It was a great success there and Brahms immediately fell in with Bülow's suggestion that he join the Meiningen orchestra on a whistle-stop tour through Europe by train, to secure maximum exposure for the work. Touring orchestras were a novelty induced by the new ease of railway communications, and some of Brahms's friends sneered at him for joining 'strolling players'. But nothing could have done Brahms more good. With the composer as a draw and the 'battling baron' von Bülow as propagandist for his cause, the concerto had been heard at Stuttgart, Zurich, Breslau, Leipzig, Hamburg, Bremen, Munster, Utrecht, Frankfurt, Kiel, Vienna and Berlin, all by the end of February.

The Herzogenbergs heard it on New Year's Day in Leipzig, where a sympathetic journal noted that the audience showed little appreciation of Brahms's importance or of his new composition. Critics elsewhere were generally bemused by this colossal work – still the largest piano concerto in the repertoire, apart from Busoni's elephantine work. Some called it chamber music writ large, others, levelling the usual charge of symphony with piano obbligato, also noticed an element of intellectual arrogance. Others, however, regarded it as the greatest of concertos, recognising the warm romanticism of its themes woven into a technically masterful framework. When it was published in 1882, it was dedicated to Brahms's 'dear friend and teacher, Eduard Marxsen'. The old man must have felt that his early faith in the gifted slum-boy had been vindicated a hundredfold.

After a brief trip to Italy in the spring of 1882, Brahms moved back to his favourite resort of Ischl. A recent performance he had attended in Vienna of Goethe's *Iphigenie auf Taurus* had brought on a severely classical mood, and he now chose the *Song of the Fates* from the play for his next choral work. The text shakes a fist at the blind and pitiless gods, and Brahms matched it with dark, uncompromising music. He dedicated it to his new friend, the Duke of Meiningen.

Having purged this mood with cathartic sounds, Brahms relaxed and turned to the intimate chamber world. He composed a cheerful string quintet in F major, Op.88, and finished his second piano trio, begun two years before. He posted the quintet to Elisabeth with the characteristically dismissive apology: 'I am sending you a little ditty.'

Clara received the trio, and after she had pronounced it 'a splendid work,' Brahms sent it to Simrock. He was especially proud of it, and wrote an uncharacteristic covering letter:

You have not received such a beautiful trio from me before, and probably have not published anything as good for ten years.

The fact that this is true does not detract from the surprise of hearing Brahms say it.

The contrasting moods of stoical defiance in the *Song of the Fates*, Op.89, and serene joy found in the chamber music were united in sketches he now began for a third symphony. But he kept very quiet about that.

October was darkened by the death of the gentle Nottebohm. Towards the end, Brahms had overcome his innate horror of illness and visited him at Graz, where he died; then he arranged the funeral, and willingly paid for it himself. But a new meeting with a young girl helped to lighten his mood. In January 1883 Brahms visited the North German town of Krefeld, where he heard the twenty-six-year-old contralto Hermine Spiess perform in his *Song of the Fates*. Meeting her afterwards, he found himself deeply attracted to her and, although she later maintained that their relationship was platonic, there is little doubt that she reciprocated some of his feelings.

After conducting his Second Symphony and appearing in the new piano concerto at the sixtieth Lower Rhine Festival in Cologne that May, he returned to Wiesbaden nearby to spend the summer close to Hermine. From the 'incredibly nice quarters', as he described the studio apartment he rented there, he could see across the roofs of the ancient town to his beloved Rhine. Here, with Hermine as his frequent companion and surrounded by the landscapes of his youth, the fifty-year-old composer reviewed his half century and completed his Third Symphony in F major, Op.90, as a testament to his beliefs.

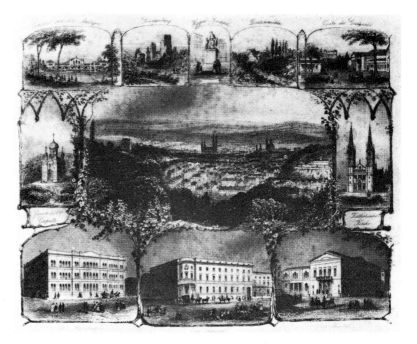

Wiesbaden, where Brahms wrote his Third Symphony.

13 Quarrels and Reconciliation

Disgustingly stale and prosy. Fundamentally false and perverse. A single cymbal-stroke of a work by Liszt expresses more intellect and emotion than all three symphonies of Brahms and his serenades taken together.

So Hugo Wolf spluttered hysterically in his *Salonblatt* review following the first performance of Brahms's new symphony in Vienna that December. The war of factions had reached an outrageous climax. Supporters of the New German camp, adopting the unassuming Bruckner as their latest champion after Wagner's death in February that year, had booed, hissed and created a fearful uproar as Hans Richter conducted the work.

Brahms, far from flinching, laughed out loud. He knew that hardly anyone paid any attention to Wolf, whose petty explosions of malice hid the spite of small talent and hinted at the padded cell in which he was eventually confined; his quizzical agnosticism was also offended by Bruckner's simple faith, which he considered 'priest-ridden', and the massive symphonies he composed, far from being a threat to his own reputation were, in Brahms's view, 'symphonic boa-constrictors', and a 'swindle' that would soon be forgotten.

Hanslick, naturally, understood. He regarded the Third Symphony as 'artistically, the most perfect of the three', uniting the 'titanic' First Symphony with the 'untroubled charm' of the Second. The most influential papers reviewed it favourably, declaring it to be the finest work Brahms had produced, which annoyed him more than anything Wolf or his clique could have said as he knew that it would provoke reaction in other towns. On playing the score through in February 1883, Clara wrote to Brahms:

What harmonious mood pervades the whole! All the movements seem to be of one piece, one beat of the heart, each one a jewel. From start to finish one is wrapped about with the mysterious charm of the woods and forests.

This at least had the merit of being a purely personal response.

Yet Brahms could afford to be inwardly indifferent to high praise and low abuse alike, for he had achieved a remarkable balance in his precarious emotions. Taking his personal motto FAF as a motto for the whole symphonic argument, in the music he reviews doubt and melancholy but achieves a sunset glow of affirmation in the final pages. The face that Widmann had seen in

120

Hans Richter, who conducted the first performance of Brahms's Third Symphony.

the garden at Pressbaum smiled benignly on the vicissitudes of his fifty years. He was still free, and probably happy.

Wherever the new symphony was played, it evoked wild enthusiasm. Joachim had met Brahms at Koblenz early in 1883, and although cool towards him, immediately offered to champion the new work when it was finished. He conducted it three times in January 1884 at Berlin. Von Bülow performed it at Meiningen twice in the same evening and Brahms took over the baton at Wiesbaden on 18 January, at Cologne, and at Leipzig in February at a concert where Hermine Spiess also sang some of his songs.

Brahms had spent more time than usual in North Germany during the previous year, and the warm reception he now received seemed to herald the return of a wanderer. Rumours circulated that he was disenchanted with Austria after attempts made by a German minority to gain supremacy in Austrian political life and involve Bismarck, and he had declared it to be virtually impossible for a German to live in Vienna any longer. Taking this as a cue, Cologne now offered him the directorship of its municipal orchestra at a very tempting salary.

Germany would clearly seem to be a place for someone as patriotic as Brahms. It had expanded into a world power with the fashionable acquisition of colonies in Africa and the South Pacific, but for all his avowed pride in his homeland and his momentary outbursts against his adopted country, Brahms was basically unforgiving. One corner of Germany had rejected him, and when he declined the Cologne offer, he brought a mention of that into his letter:

I am thinking now of Hamburg, my native city, where, since the time I consider I began to count for something, my name has repeatedly been – absolutely ignored.

And, as though to emphasise the point, he immediately went south to spend a few days on Lake Como with the Duke of Meiningen. Nostalgia then drew him back to Mürzzuschlag, the village close to Vienna where he and his father had stopped on their walking tour through Styria. His companions in this spot included the industrialist Dr Richard Fellinger and his sculptor wife, Marie, at whose house in Vienna Brahms was a frequent guest. Clara, Billroth and Hanslick also visited him during the summer months and learned that Brahms had begun another symphony. He was still there in October, writing to Clara:

It is wonderfully beautiful here and I only wish you could be with me on one of these magical moonlight evenings on the Semmering.

Dietrich tempted Brahms to Oldenburg for a Brahms festival in December, although Brahms, with his usual modesty, had initially replied on a postcard:

A Brahms evening is not exactly to my taste, but I like something like the 'Liebeswalzer' in the programme. Perhaps at the close you will give a decent piece by a decent musician.

Bowing to his request, the *Liebeslieder* waltzes appeared in the programme, with Hermine Spiess among the vocalists, but the more substantial fare included the Third Symphony and the Second Piano Concerto, which aroused 'a storm of enthusiasm', Dietrich records.

After seeing the first four Schubert symphonies (which he had edited) through the press, Brahms returned to Mürzzuschlag in the summer of 1885 to finish what was to be his last symphony, the Fourth Symphony in E minor, Op.98. It turned out to be the most strictly disciplined of the four; essentially it is a summing-up of his whole attitude towards the symphony, but its massive austerity is used to organise a questing, powerfully romantic vision of life. The most daringly original feature appears in the last movement, but this, too, is inspired by firm traditional ideas. It is a *chaconne* based on one that Bach used in his Cantata No.150. As early as 1877, Brahms had written to Clara from Pörtschach:

The chaconne is, in my opinion, one of the most wonderful and most incomprehensible pieces of music . . . If I could picture myself writing, or even conceiving such a piece, I am certain that the extreme excitement and emotional tension would have driven me mad.

And to von Bülow he had written at the same time of the Bach cantata:

What would you think of this theme used as the basis of a symphonic movement? But it would have to be altered chromatically in some way.

He did alter it slightly, and his tribute to Bach grew into a powerful, uncompromisingly assertive *passacaglia*. He was more cautious than ever, and his doubts were shared by the Herzogenbergs, usually his staunchest admirers. Elisabeth wrote to him after studying the score:

Your piece affects me curiously, the more penetration I bring to bear on it, the more impenetrable it becomes . . . I have the feeling that this work of your brain is designed too much with a view to microscopic inspection . . . as if it were a tiny world for the wise and the initiated in which the common people 'that walk in darkness' could have but a slender portion.

Hanslick, too was bemused. When he heard it in the two-piano reduction, he said: 'You know, I had the feeling I was being cudgelled by two enormously intellectual people.'

Clearly such incomprehension from his closest sympathisers called for more care than previously. Writing to von Bülow from Mürzzuschlag, Brahms showed reservations:

122

I have often . . . had a pleasing vision of rehearsing it with you in a leisurely way – a vision that I still have although I wonder if it will ever have any other audience! I rather fear it has been influenced by this climate, where the cherries never ripen. You would never touch them!

Von Bülow agreed to try the symphony out at Meiningen that autumn. The twenty-one-year-old Richard Strauss, who had just been appointed von Bülow's assistant conductor, was present, and was deeply impressed, seeing in the slow movement 'a funeral procession moving in silence across moonlit heights', though Brahms, naturally, would have no part of such 'programme' interpretation by the neo-Wagnerian Strauss.

Brahms conducted the first performance at Meiningen on 17 October. The audience, far from regarding it as academic, applauded rapturously and tried to secure an encore of its jubilant scherzo. Armed with such approval, Brahms immediately set off as 'spare conductor' with the Meiningen orchestra, touring nine towns in Germany and Holland by train. Everywhere he went the new symphony was the showpiece of the evening, and he was so delighted with its success that when the tour was over he could not be prevented from introducing it at Frankfurt, only a few days before von Bülow himself was to arrive and conduct the work. Von Bülow was deeply offended at this thoughtless piece of upstaging, and imagining that Brahms no longer had confidence in him promptly resigned his position as Meiningen's conductor. Once more, Brahms's tactlessness lost him a good friend and champion.

Joachim, though still smarting from Brahms's behaviour towards himself, secured an enthusiastic reception for the symphony in Berlin and Leipzig. Richter conducted it in Vienna

The 'brown house with green shutters' where Brahms stayed at Thun.

on 17 June 1886. Here the reception was cool, with Wolf putting in his usual jibe: 'The art of composing without ideas has found its most worthy representative in Brahms.' Even Hanslick had not entirely come to terms with the work, writing in his review, 'It is like a dark well, the longer we look into it, the more brightly the stars shine back.'

Unperturbed by such reserve, Brahms was spending the summer at Thun, near Berne, which Widmann had recommended to him the previous year. In his first-hand account of the visit, he tells us that Brahms 'rented the whole first floor of a brown house with green shutters' in order to be undisturbed. From there he could see the mountains and was particularly interested in an island promontory on the lake where Heinrich von Kleist had lived in 1802. Kleist – a real-life Werther who had shot himself and his mistress because he could not tailor his sense of destiny to the real world – had written a number of remarkable plays dealing with subconscious motives which Brahms admired greatly.

Widmann once more captures the industrious composer as he potters about:

He would rise at dawn and make himself a cup of coffee in his Viennese machine, for which a faithful admirer . . . in Marseilles had sent him excellent Mocha coffee . . . The morning hours were devoted to work, for which he always seemed to be in the right vein in this Thun residence where a large verandah and a suite of spacious rooms offered him an undisturbed walk for meditation.

His meditations turned once more to chamber music. He wrote his Second Cello Sonata in F major, Op.99, his Second Violin Sonata in A major, Op.100, and his Third Piano Trio in C minor, Op.101, that summer. All are marked with the new tautness of style and something of the harsh landscape he had faced in the Fourth Symphony. On reading the scores, the Herzogenbergs wrote back, 'We have no greater pleasure in the world than that we derive from your music'.

Brahms indulged his predilection for casual, though always spotlessly clean clothes to the full at Thun: he was frequently seen in a collarless striped flannel shirt, covered in bad weather by a brown-grey shawl held on by a huge pin. 'People gazed in astonishment,' Widmann records, adding that Brahms reminded him of the sinister and fantastic buyer of shadows and souls in Chamisso's *Peter Schlemihl* – a comparison that would have delighted Brahms, who loved the Hoffmannesque macabre.

Widmann was Brahms's chief companion that year. The railway ran direct from Thun to Berne, and Brahms travelled there every week to visit the Widmann family. Here, he would try out his new works and sift through any new books sent to Widmann for review in the journal he now edited. His reading was catholic and voracious. It included dictionaries of philology, Grillparzer's plays, Keller's novels and poems and even Stanley's

Africa, all of which he carried off in a brown leather satchel, 'like a geologist's'. He also read the philosopher Nietzsche, once such an ardent champion of Wagner and then hardly known at all. Always wary of the madness that lay close to the surface of German mysticism, Brahms distrusted his exhortations to Dionysiac ecstasy and limitless terrible joys tempered by side-swipes at the German Empire. Nietzsche and Brahms would cross swords briefly at a later date.

The fate of the German Empire was very much in Brahms's thoughts that year. In the summer of 1886 Wagner's fantastic patron, King Ludwig II of Bavaria – long certified, and confined far from even ceremonial centres of power – drowned in suspicious circumstances in the Starnbergersee. Brahms understood that the ensuing political crisis pulled a thread from the fabric of German unity for, as Widmann noted, he was:

An attentive newspaper reader and observer of all important events in politics, his chief thought being always whether the event in question would turn out a benefit or a misfortune for Germany and the German people. One can hardly fathom the depths of ardent patriotism that filled his breast.

That patriotism would be rewarded by another honour – membership of the Prussian Knight order 'Pour le Mérite' – awarded to Brahms later in the year.

Despite the political shadow, that summer was outwardly a pleasant one. Brahms made frequent visits to the Schänzli summer theatre nearby where he heard the latest Strauss operettas, and interspersed these with long and invigorating walks in the mountains. Friends, as usual, visited him, Klaus Groth among them. He felt a special sympathy for this man, whom he had first met in 1856: a Low German Robbie Burns whose *Quickborn*, written in Brahms's own dialect, had furnished the composer with several song texts. Hermine Spiess also arrived. Both men admired her. 'With my help', Brahms wrote to Widmann on one of his postcards, 'she will torture you with songs. You can either have the doors locked or invite Professor V. and Professor St. to share the agony.'

In spite of such dire warning, the songs he wrote that summer were generally agreed to be among his best. An attempt was also made to capture the testy composer on canvas. Simrock sent an artist to paint his portrait, who, knowing of his aversion to this idea, tried to sketch him unawares. Brahms saw through the ruse, however, and quietly moved out of sight of the easel.

As summer ended, Brahms made the acquaintance of Ernst Wildenbruch, whose historical plays about the German imperial dynasty he had admired at the Meiningen theatre. He found that they had much in common, including intense patriotism and a love of tradition, and they spent several agreeable hours in each other's company.

Yet for all his outward ease a mood of sadness, disagreement and almost paranoia seemed to darken these days. Both Liszt and Fritz Brahms had died recently, and although he had not got on too well with either, their deaths depressed him deeply. There was bad feeling and a hiatus in correspondence with both Clara and Elisabeth over imaginary difficulties stirred up by a gossip. Although their differences were soon patched up, it was an indication of the kind of person Brahms was becoming in his dealings with old friends and casual acquaintances alike. His rudeness was apparent rather than real, but his lack of tact was more serious than his short temper. It had already led to estrangements from Joachim, von Bülow, and Levi, whom he considered 'too Wagnerian', and was to claim many more good friends as he grew more irascible.

Sensing his vulnerability and isolation and knowing that journalists, autograph hunters and biographers who were not as sympathetic as Kalbeck were on the scent of every public and private utterance he made, he decided to cheat them all. That autumn, on his return to Vienna, he burned many manuscripts, letters and other private papers. He returned most of Clara's letters and pressed her to do the same with his. He also asked for the return of several early manuscripts in the possession of old friends, such as the Giessemans, so that he could destroy them. He was at Rudesheim in early 1887 when he received his letters from Clara and he immediately threw them, unopened, into the Rhine. With a shift towards appropriate symbolism, he had chosen the river that flows through the legends he adored, by whose side he had first loved Clara and in whose waters Schumann had tried to make an end of himself, to swallow up that corner of his youth for ever.

There were always new people to take the place of those friends who knew too much about him. Widmann grew closer, and Eusebius Mandyczewski, the young librarian of the Vienna Philharmonic Society archives, who had replaced Pohl when he died early in the year. He became a valued companion who would cheerfully take on the onerous tasks of copying Brahms's precious manuscripts and dispatching them to publishers and friends in registered parcels instead of the waste paper, Strauss waltzes and old string the impatient Brahms preferred. In 1886 he had engineered the honorary post of president of the Viennese Society for Musical Artists for Brahms, and the composer spent much of his time there, either at social gatherings or on gentle strolls round the Viennese countryside with its members.

Old friends sometimes drifted back when Brahms made some half-gesture of reconciliation. He regained von Bülow that year by leaving his card at the conductor's hotel in Vienna. Notes from *The Magic Flute* alluding to Pamino's cry 'Shall I see you no more', were scribbled on it. Von Bülow instantly recognised this muted apology, and Brahms and he were seen strolling round the Prater arm-in-arm that evening.

Brahms tried the same trick on Joachim. He had included a reference to the words 'Come soon' from one of his songs in the texture of the Second Violin Sonata, but this was really too cryptic, and Joachim was not to be so easily won over. He next tried associating more closely with Robert Hausmann, the cellist in Joachim's quartet. It was Hausmann who, with Brahms, had first played the Cello Sonata in F major on 24 November 1886; but that too led nowhere. After a brief trip round northern Italy in the spring of 1887 with Simrock and Kirchner ('not a day passed which was not full of the most beautiful experiences', he wrote to Clara), Brahms returned to Thun with a more ambitious idea that would involve both Hausmann and Joachim in a work of reconciliation. He wrote to Clara:

I have had the amusing idea of composing a concerto for violin and cello. If it is at all successful it might give us some fun. You can well imagine the sort of pranks one can play in such a case. But do not imagine too much!

His characteristic bluffheartiness hid the deeper motive, for although he had considered writing a second violin concerto, the inclusion of a cello part softened the apology. It was just as much a gesture of goodwill, but did not concede that the blame for the long separation between Joachim and himself was entirely Brahms's fault.

Hanslick, Kalbeck and other friends visited him and he went to see Widmann in Berne as frequently as before, but it was a cold and wet season and his mountaineering walks were severely curtailed. Hearing that Widmann was braving the weather to visit his mountain house at Meiligen, Brahms sent him a postcard:

I imagine you will take a photographer with you . . . in order to have groups taken of the frozen people . . . Afterwards we will search for newly formed ice-grottoes and finally – for the remains of the provisions!
Heartiest greeting and sympathy, your J.B.

But it was not all bad. Brahms was able to make several excursions into the mountains with Widmann, and on the last of these they reached the high Grindelwald glacier. There they lost Widmann's terrier, Argos. Brahms was greatly affected by this, saying, 'You will never see the dear little fellow again!'; but when the dog limped back to Berne unaided several days later, Brahms was as amazed as he was overjoyed: 'So, such things do happen, and are not only sportsmen's stories!', he exclaimed, and his first thought on returning to Vienna was of the dog. He wrote: 'How is Argos? Would he take it as a tender greeting from me if you were to give him a nice piece of meat, instead of a dog biscuit?'

Brahms spent part of the autumn in Baden-Baden with Clara. Joachim and Hausmann were also there and they tried out Brahms's newest compositions. Apart from the passionate *Gypsy Songs* for vocal quartet and piano, Op.103, which he had written to Hungarian texts translated by his friend Hugo Conrat, which Clara particularly enjoyed ('I am quite delighted with them. How original they are and how full of freshness, charm and passion,' she said), there was the concerto. Clara realised the message that lay behind the music at once, and wrote in her diary: 'This concerto could be seen as a work of reconciliation – Joachim and Brahms have spoken to each other again after years of silence.'

Joachim offered his old friend advice on bowing, just as he had done with the Violin Concerto. Brahms, dangerously stubborn to the last, however, totally ignored everything Joachim suggested.

When the work was first performed publicly in Cologne on 18 October, it was coolly received. Some of its hearers were disappointed, thinking the delicate balance between the instruments had muted Brahms's style; others levelled the usual charge of symphony-concerto at the work, and were not far wrong, for the layout harks back to the *sinfonia concertante* style of Brahms's beloved eighteenth century.

Whatever the reception, one feels sure Brahms would not have been discouraged. The work was performed soon after in Meiningen, Frankfurt and Basel, setting a seal on the reconciliation between Brahms and Joachim. Although neither would ever regain the wholehearted trust of their heady youth, they would never quarrel again. Brahms, who could see so many old friends slipping away through illness, death or simply disagreement, now needed all the friends he could keep.

14 Return of the Native

The Concerto in A minor for Violin, Cello and Orchestra, Op.102, was to be Brahms's last purely orchestral work. In keeping with the more relaxed tenor of his daily life, he now turned more to the intimate field of chamber music, piano pieces and songs.

The bachelor had settled immovably. A crisis concerning his apartment had been solved the previous year when Frau Truxa, the widow of a writer, and her two boys had moved into the rest of Karlsgasse 4 to keep house for the hopelessly undomesticated man. The only concessions he made to his increased status in the world were curtains in his study and an extra room to house his enormous collection of rare books and manuscripts; otherwise, he seemed careless of his surroundings. A functional bedroom with bed and washstand, a study with a bust of Beethoven, a photograph of Bismarck wreathed in triumphant laurel, a piano,

Brahms in his study at 4 Karlsgasse. Beethoven's bust looks down, Bismarck's portrait is wreathed in triumphant laurel, and the rocking chair is poised to tip unwary visitors onto the floor.

Brahms walking to the 'Red Hedgehog' – a silhouette by Otto Böhler.

Peter Ilyich Tchaikovsky. Brahms did not warm to him.

desk and rocking-chair that he had arranged to tip unwary visitors onto the floor – these were the spartan furnishings of his other two rooms.

The Viennese could almost set their watches by his movements: theatre- and concert-going, walks in the Prater where all the *filles de joie* would greet the 'Herr Doktor' happily, meals taken regularly with close friends in the back room of the convivial Red Hedgehog, where his food was lovingly prepared and a cask of Hungarian wine kept for his private consumption. His friends still included Billroth, who was his companion on many evenings, and the faithful Fellingers, who could always be relied on to provide an excellent Sunday lunch. He was also a member of the group of satirists and journalists who called themselves 'The Committee of Scoffers' and spent their leisure time in hard-drinking buffoonery, lampooning all and sundry, including, as often as not, themselves. He had grown 'very stout' according to Florence May, who visited him that year: 'He looked an old man, his hair was nearly white,' but 'he wore the happy, sunshiny look of one who had realised his purpose and was content with his share in life.' As such, he was more *Beidermeir* than Beethoven: his music reflected that artistic movement in its calm and comfortable celebration of bourgeois values now that he had come to terms with himself.

He still enjoyed visiting other musical centres, where he would occasionally take the baton or sit down at the piano in performances of his own works. On one such tour, after travelling to Hungary and Meiningen, he visited Leipzig to hear a performance of the Double Concerto with Joachim and Hausmann in the Gewandhaus on New Year's Day 1888. Staying at the house of Adolph Brodsky, who was a fervent champion of his Violin Concerto, he was introduced to Grieg and Tchaikovsky. Tchaikovsky warmed to Brahms at first, describing him in his diary as 'a good-looking man, rather short and stout', who reminded him of a 'kindly, aged Russian priest'. Brahms, however, did not warm to the neurotic Tchaikovsky. He heard a performance of his First Suite for orchestra at another Gewandhaus concert and, although polite, gave the distinct impression that he found the music self-indulgent. Tchaikovsky, too, changed his mind about Brahms, describing him later as a 'self-conscious mediocrity', and found that, during the few days he spent with the composer, they were 'ill at ease, because we do not really like each other'. Brahms and Grieg got on extremely well, however. Brahms, who had often used folk-song in his music, was particularly interested in the Norwegian's use of the music of his own land.

Another guest present at Adolph Brodsky's was the English composer Ethel Smyth, a former pupil of Heinrich von Herzogenberg and a bright spark of whom Elisabeth had written enthusiastically to Brahms. She had not yet developed into the tweedy feminist who would eventually be imprisoned for breaking windows at the Colonial Office in London, but Brahms found her

Edvard Grieg, who had more in common with Brahms.

Kaiser Whilhelm II, the new focus of Brahms's patriotism.

daunting, an impression not helped by her habit of leaping suddenly over chairs. She, for her part, was not impressed by Brahms's attitude to women and seemed to regard him as a prototype male chauvinist pig. Her view of men was, however, more biased than Brahms's view of women.

Nietzsche reappeared at this time to curry Brahms's favour. He had fallen out with Wagner in 1878 when he had defended Brahms in front of his idol, and had been asked to leave the house as a result. Now, five years after Wagner's death, he sent Brahms one of his own choral compositions, *A Hymn to Life*, with a dedication. Brahms, who secretly found the music embarrassing and banal, telling Elisabeth 'not to waste the precious daylight too often by reading such things', declined the acknowledgement politely on a visiting-card.

On 9 March Brahms heard devastating news. Kaiser Wilhelm I had died. Brahms wrote immediately to Elisabeth:

I have been much affected by the startling events in Germany. It is all on a scale – a tragic scale – unparalleled in history.

We should not be startled by his reaction. He knew that the fledgling German Empire was held together by the personalities of Bismarck and the old Kaiser. The new liberal Kaiser Frederick III was dangerously ill with cancer and he feared his early death might put the whole structure in the balance. In fact he died a mere three months later, but his son Wilhelm II immediately took firm control. This seemed to satisfy Brahms, who would not live to see this dangerously unbalanced military autocrat bring about the downfall of Germany in 1918.

Brahms had recovered sufficiently from the political shock to embark on another Italian trip in May. This time, his travelling companion was Widmann, 'the most delightful of companions', as Brahms told Clara. They were ideally suited, as both enjoyed the same leisurely pace and preferred to stay at small, obscure *pensiones* rather than the large tourist hotels where Brahms would have been the centre of too much unwelcome fuss.

Widmann's detailed account of the journey tells us that the two met at Verona on Brahms's fifty-fifth birthday, then travelled to Bologna where they visited an exhibition of rare musical manuscripts. Scores of *Fidelio* and *The Magic Flute* delighted the antiquarian Brahms, though his fondness for resurrecting the past did not extend to another part of the festivities: a concert played on ancient instruments, including a *viol d'amore*, in the presence of the Queen of Italy. This was indeed a rarity, but also a fiasco, as Brahms had predicted: 'thin, squeaking and chirping' Widmann records, 'the court ladies began to titter, and the whole performance became a farcical comedy.'

Before leaving Bologna, Brahms was paid an unexpected compliment. Martucci, the director of the Bolognese opera, who had recently conducted Brahms's Second Symphony in Naples,

Friedrich Nietzsche: Brahms snubbed him and was subsequently insulted in a pamphlet.

visited the composer at his hotel. No sooner had Martucci arrived than he prostrated himself on the ground, then, rising, began singing aloud themes from Brahms's works, finding that they had no common language. Brahms, who would normally have been greatly embarrassed by such a display, was so impressed by Martucci's sincerity that he fell in with the spirit of the occasion and enjoyed a pleasant hour, singing themes and conversing in gestures and broken Italian.

After such gratifying homage, Brahms and Widmann paid homage to another composer whose home town of Pesaro they passed on the train. Although they did not alight, each sang an aria from Rossini's *Barber of Seville*. Stopping at Loreto, they watched a procession of pilgrims arriving at the Casa Santa Lauretana shrine on their knees, singing and weeping with devotion. Brahms may have been a gruff unbeliever, but he was always courteous enough to genuflect in Catholic churches, and this simple faith and pure devotion affected him greatly. His outlook was a fine contrast to the attitudes of the priests, who stood by indifferently and dismissed their flock as 'stupid people' from the Abruzzi villages.

In Rome, Brahms tramped tirelessly round the sights, and was delighted to be mistaken for a famous German archaeologist by a souvenir vendor. While there, he and Widmann paid homage visits to the 'Genio' café near the Trevi fountain where his dead friend Feuerbach and his followers had gathered years before. They also sought out scenes in and around Rome that Feuerbach had painted, and on such visits, Widmann records, Brahms made friends with the local children who warmed to his rudimentary Italian and pockets full of sweets, following him around 'like faithful dogs'.

They returned to Thun together via Milan, Turin and the St Gothard Pass. On the whole, it had been a most agreeable journey. 'We suffered not a moment's annoyance,' Brahms wrote to Clara. 'The only insects we saw were the most beautiful glow worms.'

Earlier in the year, hearing that the Herzogenbergs were both ill, Brahms had put his house at Thun at their 'immediate disposal', selflessly offering to take up lodgings nearby. They had declined the offer, so he was able to return to his favourite spot. But two sources of annoyance awaited him. In his absence, a promenade had been built along the River Aare immediately below his window, and now tourists would gather to listen when he played the piano. As if this were not enough, he found that Nietzsche had taken his revenge for the snub Brahms had inflicted on him. In his latest book, *The Case of Wagner*, published in May, although aiming most of his darts at Wagner, Nietzsche also found space to insult Brahms, calling him 'the eunuch of music' whose compositions enshrined the 'melancholy of impotence'. This was a more reasoned charge than the ravings of Wagner against Brahms, and Brahms was momentarily cast down by it. Elisabeth read the book and wrote to him: 'Really, this man's vanity will bring him to a lunatic asylum yet.' These were prophetic words, but it was no consolation to Brahms to learn a year later that the brilliant and solitary philosopher had, indeed, been committed to an asylum, another genius struck down by the dangerous imbalance of a thoroughly romantic mind; and he would have loathed the ultimate madness awaiting his writings: less than forty years after his death they were distorted into an obscene patina of philosophy for the horrors of the Nazi régime.

Melancholy, but not impotence, may be found in the Third Violin Sonata in D minor, Op.108, which Brahms completed at Thun that summer. It is the largest of the violin sonatas, almost symphonic in its broad design, and if there is undeniable sadness in its themes, there is also power and passionate drama. Smarting from Nietzsche's diatribe, he was more self-critical than usual and canvassed the opinions of all his closest friends on its worth. They were unanimous in their praise. 'What a wonderfully beautiful thing you have given us,' Clara wrote, and Brahms, reassured, dedicated it to von Bülow in another gesture of reconciliation.

Although he continued to enjoy Widmann's hospitality in Berne during the summer, an article Widmann had carelessly written as temporary political editor on his journal, criticising Wilhelm II, provoked a bitter argument between them in August. At the height of it, perhaps also remembering Nietzsche's castigation of the German Empire as the 'triumph of philistinism', Brahms wrote to Widmann from Thun:

All that comes from Germany is secretly criticised though the Germans themselves lead the way. It is the same in Politics as in Art. If the Bayreuth Theatre stood in France, it would not require anything so great as the works of Wagner to make you . . . and all the world go on a pilgrimage thither, and rouse your enthusiasm for something so ideally conceived and executed as those music-dramas.

When Wagner had died, Brahms told the orchestra that he was conducting, 'A master is dead, we shall rehearse no more today.' With these and many other remarks he made at other times, it is obvious that he bore no real grudge against his chief rival. The fault lay with those factions and musical opinions that forced the two leading German composers of their age into public opposition, a narrow view that could not see they were really part of the same musical process.

The political quarrel . . . embittered our next meetings, as, leaving aside the original theme of contention, we had embarked on useless discussions on the advantages and disadvantages of the monarchical and republican forms of government.

So Widmann found that an open breach was imminent with his friend. He appealed to their mutual friend, the novelist Gottfried Keller, to mediate. In reply, he wrote to Widmann:

The very son of a free town clings more pathetically to emperor and

133

dynasty than probably was ever the case in the days of former greatness. At the same time, I must confess that you did injustice to the royal speaker . . . in your article.

By then, however, the worst was over. 'Good fellowship was again established,' Widmann says, and shortly afterwards, Brahms left Thun to stay with Clara at Baden-Baden.

He found her in difficulties once more. Her troubles seemed to Brahms to be never-ending and more than once he hints in his letters to her that she seemed marked down by Fate. Now he learned that her extended family was hard put to make ends meet. She herself had virtually ceased to perform in public as her arm grew worse, so could not help. As tactfully as he was able, Brahms wrote to her on his return to Vienna, pressing her to accept a gift of 10,000 marks, calling it 'a belated contribution to the Schumann Fund . . . to disburden myself of some of my superfluous pelf'. Although she refused, he sent the money anyway, only stipulating, as with all his gifts, that it should not be made common knowledge.

Christmas in Vienna was a merrier occasion that year. Brahms set up Frau Truxa's Christmas tree in his library – the first time this annual ritual occurred – and delighted in giving presents to her two children, who had already begun to call him 'Uncle Bahms' (sic). This latest adopted family would eventually give him the surrogate pleasure of the real family for which he had always longed. After Christmas he visited Meiningen, where Joachim and Hausmann performed the Double Concerto again and Brahms once more enjoyed dressing up for the hospitality of his two aristocratic friends. After Joachim had performed the new violin sonata in Vienna, Brahms joined him in Berlin for his Jubilee concert which he described to Clara as 'very dignified and beautiful', then he paid a fleeting visit to Hamburg where he saw his stepmother and her son, and visited his sister in her 'charming home'.

In the spring of 1889 Clara at last made the visit to Italy that Brahms had long advised her to undertake. She stayed with the Herzogenbergs in Florence. Heinrich had just undergone a painful operation that left his leg and neck stiff, and Elisabeth was suffering from the onset of the heart disease that would eventually kill her, but they both had sympathy to spare for Clara, and Elisabeth sent Brahms a sad description of the old lady's condition:

The dear thing has ten years too many on her shoulders. Once or twice we found her miserably seated on her camp-stool before some Signorelli or Verocchio, rubbing her hands nervously and trying so hard to feel some enthusiasm. But nothing would come and carry her off her feet.

Brahms replied that he was sorry that the trip 'fell so far short of what one hoped and desired for her'. Seeing her like this might

have made him secretly glad that he had not married her in his youth. Their relationship, if it had survived, would then have reached the same crisis as that of his own father and mother, their age difference being almost exactly the same.

Elisabeth's letter reached him at Ischl. The new promenade had turned him against his old house at Thun, and the open political hostility between Switzerland and Germany would have made a prolonged visit there very uncomfortable and might have sparked off more arguments with Widmann. Now he was glad to return to the fashionable resort where he had so many good friends. It was a decision he never altered, and Ischl became his summer home for the rest of his life.

Once more he took his old apartment. The Hotel Kaiserin Elisabeth where he dined, and Walter's coffee house where he read the papers, were delighted to see him again. He regretted that no train ran to Berne, so that trips to the Widmanns' ceased, but he made up for this by visiting Billroth: an hour by boat or train would take him to his lakeside villa in St Gilgen. Gmunden was also close and he often stayed there with Victor von Miller and his family, who kept open house to Brahms and all his friends. The von Millers were such great admirers that they established a Brahms museum at Gmunden after the composer's death, containing mementos set in an exact replica of Brahms's rooms at Ischl, right

135

Brahms at Ischl with Johann Strauss, his host for many glittering parties.

down to the window frames. The Johann Strauss villa was once more the scene of many glittering parties, and at one gathering, it is said, Brahms signed the fan of Strauss's stepdaughter with a quotation from the *Blue Danube* waltz, writing underneath, 'Unfortunately not by Johannes Brahms'.

While at Ischl, Brahms received news of two new honours: the Order of Leopold from Austria and, more treasured than this, the Freedom of the City of Hamburg. Hans von Bülow, in his capacity as resident conductor there, had persuaded Burgomaster Petersen to confer this on Brahms, despite diehards on the council still opposed to the slum-boy who had dared to rise above his background. Brahms wrote proudly to Clara:

The distinction is a rare one. I am number thirteen. The first were Blücher and Tennenborn, the last Bismarck and Molkte.

He immediately sat down to compose a choral work especially for the occasion: 'Something suitable for a national festival or commemoration . . . with glorious scriptural texts,' he wrote to Clara. The *Festival and Commemoration Sentences*, Op.109, that resulted did indeed reflect patriotism in their texts, but with a warning that the felicity of the nation must not be taken for granted. Still in the choral mood, he also composed his Three Motets, Op.110. Unlike the public and expansive *Festival Sentences*, they are bleak and uncompromising works in Brahms's most spiritual vein. But he did not take this mood too seriously. When he sent the Motets to the Herzogenbergs later in the year, he used copies of gay Viennese dance music to wrap them up.

That summer, Simrock also gave him the unprecedented opportunity to rewrite an early work. He was republishing the

The concert hall at Hamburg: Brahms was given the Freedom of the City in 1889.

Piano Trio No.1 in B major, Op.8, a work that Brahms had long wanted to alter. As he later wrote to Clara:

With what childish amusement I whiled away the beautiful summer days you will never guess. I have rewritten my B major trio and can call it Op.108 instead of Op.8. It will not be so wild as it was before – but whether it will be better – ?

Universal opinion agrees that it is better: the mature composer took his 'wild' young self in hand that summer, although he did not alter any of his broad, passionate melodies. In the end, he told Simrock to publish both versions together under the original opus number, but it is his later version that has been played more frequently ever since.

He interrupted his stay at Ischl in July to receive his freedom in Hamburg. On his return he wrote to Clara:

All that happened before, during and after the ceremony was as pleasant as the fact itself. My first thought on such occasions is of my father and the wish that he might have been there.

The occasion did not arise for a performance of the *Festival*

Brahms the celebrity.

Sentences, so he returned to Hamburg in September to conduct it at an exhibition of Commerce and Industry. Hamburg had now grown into the chief port serving the new industrial might of Germany and it was anxious to show off its supremacy, yet Brahms did not feel out of place in this showcase of materialism for he saw it as another facet of patriotism. The Hamburg Cecilia Society performed the *Festival and Commemoration Sentences* in exactly the right circumstances, and they were enthusiastically received. He dedicated the new work to Burgomaster Petersen, and became so friendly with his family that he stayed at their home outside the city several times. Brahms and Hamburg were finally reconciled.

At the end of the year an event occurred that links the last classical master with our own age in a curiously intimate way. In November, Brahms wrote to Clara from Vienna:

Brahms at the Fellingers' house. Dr Fellinger and his wife are seated to Brahms's right.

At the present moment we are living under the shadow of the phonograph and I have had the opportunity of hearing it often and quite pleasantly . . . It is like being in fairyland again. Tomorrow evening, Dr Fellinger will have it at his home.

That evening, during one of his regular visits to the Fellingers', Brahms met Theodore Wangemann, Thomas Edison's European agent, who was collecting the voices of famous men and women. Brahms, who was always fascinated by new inventions, turned delightedly to the primitive trumpet of his cylinder recording machine and said:

Grüsse an Herrn Doktor Edison. I am Doctor Brahms. Johannes Brahms.

His voice squeaks in German and, complimenting the inventor, in broken English through a storm of surface sound, then there follows a minute of Brahms at the piano playing an excerpt from his Hungarian Dance No. 1, and that is all. It is the only recording of Brahms that exists: a tantalising glimpse that, linked to his name, has the resonance of legend as though Beethoven or another of the great classical masters had spoken and played to us from the past. Yet the invention was then little more than a toy, and it is doubtful whether Brahms realised that it would one day carry his music further and more quickly than any of his own exhausting concert tours.

139

15 A Sunset Glow

One last flirtation – if it can be so called – dates from the beginning of 1890. Brahms met another contralto, Alice Barbi, and the friendship between the young girl and the fifty-six-year-old composer ripened and continued even after she married two years later. He was often seen in public with her, and acted as her accompanist when she sang his songs. 'It would be impossible to hear anything more lovely,' he wrote to Clara in March of that year.

That same month, the brash young Kaiser, tired of his grandfather's chief minister and desiring what he called 'personal rule' to expand Germany into a war machine, engineered Bismarck's resignation. Brahms and his closest friends were all shocked, Elisabeth writing that she was, 'nonplussed by the recent turn of events and the attitude of the Almighty in countenancing them'. A Bismarck admiration society, in which Brahms was interested, even wanted to register its disapproval by meeting the architect of German unity in Berlin and pulling his coach through the streets, but Brahms, although deeply moved by the fall of his idol, was not involved in exhibitionism of this order.

Shortly afterwards Widmann met him at Riva to accompany him on another Italian journey. The composer, who had travelled all night by train from Vienna, was wearing three pairs of trousers to keep out the cold. 'Such practical inspirations put him into a happy mood for the whole day,' Widmann asserts. 'Possessing great dexterity with the railway guide', Brahms had planned a shorter trip than formerly. They visited Parma, where Brahms was deeply moved by Parmigiano's 'Betrothal of St Catherine' with its 'many indescribably lovely faces of fair-haired children'. They next stayed at Cremona, famous for violins and Monteverdi. Their host's son at the inn was a barber and violinist like Figaro, and this amused Brahms greatly. Brahms also discovered a statue to St Joachim in his wanderings and thought it 'quite fitting' that there should be a monument to his friend in the city of violins. On Easter Day the two attended a choral mass composed by one Andreotti — 'a man of such small stature that he hardly reached up to an ordinary table'. Brahms remarked dryly that 'his melodies were surprisingly cheerful' in the circumstances.

On the return they stopped at Padua where Brahms was pleased to see an edition of his piano sonatas in a shop window, thence back to Verona where Brahms moved on to Vienna alone. He did not stay there long, but was soon installed in Ischl for the rest of

Cremona, the city of violins.

the summer. Here he wrote the joyous String Quintet No.2 in G major, Op.111, a work so fresh and positive that after a rehearsal in Vienna later that year, a friend suggested calling it 'Brahms on the Prater'. 'You've hit it,' Brahms replied, 'and all the pretty girls there, eh?' Elisabeth, who was ill and depressed when she received the score, wrote to Brahms: 'Reading it was like feeling spring breezes.'

At this point, Brahms decided that he had done his best work and, with that strength of critical will that had marked his whole career, announced that he would retire and write no other new works. Perhaps he thought that life should be enjoyed now without the pressures of maintaining a reputation, for an air of frivolity may be found in this letter written to the Herzogenbergs early in 1891:

Brahms in his customary
stride.

I look at your . . . pleasant circle of serious-minded, seriously interested people with envious approval. Unfortunately, one or other of you is always having to lie up!

The truth of the matter was that he had simply retired from the clamour of public demands, putting away the mask of Beethoven's heir and entering a benign, autumnal world of secret thoughts and stoical certainties. A last period of composition was about to begin, more intimate, less constrained than before; some would say, more genuinely Brahms.

It was Meiningen that stirred his creative pulse once again. He stayed there in March 1891, and Widmann, who was also present to try out his tragedy, *Oenone*, at the ducal theatre, speaks of the 'almost Olympian cheerfulness' that shone in Brahms's eyes during this time: 'These days . . . were bathed in sunshine as in the Golden Age,' he recalls. Brahms's delight in the castle may be seen in the account he wrote to Clara of his visit:

When you are there you can make yourself at home in every way. You can, if you like, have your meals sent up to your room at midday or in the evening . . . The suites we . . . occupy are not only exceedingly beautiful and luxurious but also as comfortable as you can possibly imagine. Particularly pleasant is the lavish supply of candles and lamps and the outlook on the park.

Music was played from morning to night, often going on after midnight in the duke's private apartments. At one concert, Brahms first heard Richard Mühlfeld, the virtuoso clarinettist of the Meiningen orchestra, playing a clarinet concerto by Weber. 'You have never heard such a clarinet player,' Brahms wrote to Clara, 'he is absolutely the best I know.' So impressed was he that, despite his 'retirement', he spent time at Ischl that summer writing two works especially for Mühlfeld: the sad little Clarinet Trio in A minor, Op.114, and the glorious but equally melancholy Clarinet Quintet in B minor, Op.115. 'Every day our world grows emptier,' Clara had written to him after the death of her son Ferdinand in June, and the music seems to reflect on life's transience. Yet its sadness is chastened by a warm serenity, and nothing Brahms ever wrote expresses this mellow mood so well.

Brahms had much to lower his spirits. Relations with Clara were strained. Her nervous condition made her so irritable that when Brahms had paid her a brief visit in March 'it was like a nightmare,' she confided in her diary. In October, they quarrelled openly. Brahms had aided the printing of Schumann's Fourth Symphony in its original version, which he thought superior to the heavily orchestrated revision. Clara disagreed. Only with supreme tact did Brahms calm the neurotic Clara, and the quarrel left a feeling of bitterness and exclusion in Brahms's mind that festered for at least another year.

Then, on 7 January 1892, Elisabeth died in Italy of the heart disease that had incapacitated her for so long. She was only forty-four. 'You know how unutterably I myself suffer by the loss of your beloved wife,' Brahms wrote to Heinrich, and this was no form of words. Although relations between them had grown more reserved since both the Herzogenbergs fell ill, and Brahms had shrunk from contact with such reminders of human frailty, he was to keep a photograph of Elisabeth on his desk until his own death, and deeply missed the warm, frank, intelligent letters she had sent him for twenty-five years.

Then, on 11 June, his sister died after a long illness. Brahms had been with her in Hamburg at the end: 'We who were watching could not help wishing for the end long ago, for in her case it was only a release,' he wrote stoically to Clara. 'Thus, one after another, our loved ones go and the wilderness about our hearts increases,' Clara replied, alluding to the words Brahms had set in his *Alto Rhapsody* more than twenty years before.

Something of his mood of loss, but also resignation in the face of it, was carried over to the piano pieces he composed at Ischl that year. Although some were almost certainly written earlier and are opulently scored in his most confident vein, the quiet and intimate numbers from the Six Fantaisies, Op.116, were most probably inspired by seeing some of Elisabeth's own short piano pieces for the first time. Here, the pianist-composer is heard in a reflective mood, almost improvising as his thoughts run on his sister and his dearest friends. The same mood is found in the Three Intermezzi, Op.117, also finished that year. He called the first 'a lullaby of my sorrows'.

Brahms, who loved the lamp-lit ambience of Meiningen and always wrote when possible with a quill, was not too pleased with the addition he found in his flat on his return from Ischl. 'Despite all my protestations, they have installed electric light in my rooms,' he wrote to Clara in dismay, although he did not tell the Fellingers, who had caused the work to be carried out, that its harsh glare was an intrusion.

In September, his friendship with Clara was at last put on a firm footing again, but not without Brahms admitting that he had been tactless, and reiterating:

You and your husband constitute the most beautiful experience of my life, and represent all that is richest and most noble in it.

Clara replied coldly:

Personal intercourse with you is often difficult and yet my friendship for you has always helped to rise above your vagaries.

Brahms sent her his new piano pieces. Clara approved. Brahms wrote again in December reminding her of the last Christmas they had spent together:

That evening, the brightly lighted tree shone forth and all eyes, young

See Geiringer
at p.157 !

?

144

and old, reflected its glory . . . I am going to start work on the Christmas tree and think of you as I am doing so.

Clara melted, and the two old friends grew close once more. The letters between them took on a tone of intimacy not seen since the early days, when Brahms had loved her passionately. He even decorated them with whimsical drawings of insects and birds as he had done then.

After visiting Meiningen in January 1893, where Widmann and he had great fun staging Widmann's dramatic parody on Nietzsche's *Beyond Good and Evil*, Brahms visited Hamburg to clear up the last details of his sister's estate. 'Any homesickness that I might have felt was completely washed away by the genuine Hamburg weather which was my lot,' he opined to Clara, but consoled himself with the thought of southern skies: 'I am planning . . . a trip to Sicily.' Meanwhile, Clara had heard Mühlfeld play the Clarinet Quintet:

What a magnificent thing it is and how it moves one! How the subtle fusion of the instruments with the soft and insistent wail of the clarinet above them lays hold on one . . . [Mühlfeld] might have been specially created for your works.

Brahms made his escape to Italy just in time that year, for his sixtieth birthday was imminent. All manner of official fuss was planned, and he knew it. With Friedrich Hegar, the pianist Robert Freund and the indefatigable Widmann as chronicler, he set off for Genoa to embark on a ship bound for Naples. But arriving there on 16 April, they found that the only ship available was Hungarian. Brahms, nervous of the sea at the best of times, remarked that he knew the Bohemians were a seafaring nation according to *The Winter's Tale*, but no one had made that claim for the Hungarians. Dissuaded by his little joke, everyone went by train.

Hanslick was staying near Naples, at Sorrento, and they recovered from the hot, dusty journey by sitting in his orange-grove one afternoon drinking Chianti and watching dolphins playing in the Bay of Naples below. Suitably soothed, Brahms was at last persuaded to board a steamer for Sicily. Widmann tells us:

Brahms was able, for the first time, to enjoy the peculiar charm of a night voyage. Behind the ship was a track of phosphorescent ripples out of which fantastic shapes appeared now and again to flash into sight. Then came the wonderful sunrise.

Brahms was in his element in Sicily. Widmann again:

What pleasure he took in scanning the romantic scenes painted in bright colours upon the two-wheeled carts, especially if these pictures recalled episodes in the poems of Ariosto or Tasso.

145

The Bay of Naples.

At Girgenti they stayed at a small *albergo* overlooking 'the steep descent to the plain and the wonderful ancient temples by the sea'. Visiting the Temple of Juno next day, Widmann saw Brahms with 'his bare head and silvery beard illuminated by the morning sun' as the seventy-year-old Grecian tragic poet, who according to legend had been killed by a tortoise dropped from an eagle's claws on that same spot.

At Syracuse, Brahms visited the grave of another poet, the German exile August von Platen whose poems he had set and whose austere classicism struck a chord in his own make-up at this time. In Taormina, which was Brahms's 'especial favourite', they visited the ancient Saracen city of Mola 'perched on rocky pinnacles'. Although he was not as energetic as he had been, Brahms could still keep up a good pace on foot: 'uphill walking was rather a difficulty . . . but his downhill pace resembled that of a rolling ball.'

Boarding a ship in Messina harbour to make the return voyage to Naples, Widmann caught his foot in an iron ring and broke it, so Brahms spent his sixtieth birthday at his friend's bedside in Naples, as far from public fuss as it was possible to be. Congratulations arrived by letter and telegram all day long, nevertheless. Friends from Vienna, the Duke of Meiningen, and many others joined in the 'fuss'. 'I can only hope you are dreaming the day away or celebrating it merrily amid the glories of nature,'

146

Clara wrote, and a telegram from the Vienna Conservatoire congratulating him on his *seventieth* birthday was returned with Brahms's annotation: 'Not accepted; I protest!'

Having seen Widmann comfortably seated on a train bound for Berne, Brahms returned with Freund and Hegar, stopping at Rome – where he was delighted to observe preparations for the visit of Kaiser Wilhelm II – and Venice. This was to be Brahms's last visit to Italy. Despite his expressing a desire to return several times in the next three years, no one was able to make the journey with him. 'I find travelling companions essential,' he had once said, and he would not travel alone.

Back in Vienna, he found that the Philharmonic Society had struck a limited edition of bronze medals with his likeness raised in relief to celebrate his age. Although he was flattered by this gesture, he was characteristically peeved that he had to read the mountain of congratulatory letters and telegrams that had arrived in his absence.

At Ischl that summer, he returned to the piano and composed the Six Pieces, Op.118 and the Four Pieces, Op.119. On receiving them, Clara wrote in her diary:

It really is marvellous how things pour from him; it is wonderful how he combines passion and tenderness in the smallest of spaces.

Indeed, concentration is the key to these pieces. A passionate heart is troubled by bleak stoicism and restlessness and makes the set as remarkable as its companions of the previous year. Once more, Brahms writes in quiet, confessional tones for his ear alone, although he also had the ailing Clara in mind: 'I have just finished a little piece that will at least suit your fingers,' he had written to her of Op.119. The neuralgia in her arm was ever-present, but she could still manage to play through these 'pearls', as she called them.

Despite these late masterpieces, music had now become Brahms's hobby, rather than his career. Inspired by Alice Barbi's love of folk-song, he now began lovingly comparing variants and annotating the large number of folk-songs he had collected throughout his life, the first set being ready for publication that year.

In February 1894, he lost two of his oldest friends, Billroth and von Bülow, within six days of each other. After Billroth's death, he wrote stoically to Clara: 'His death had been long expected and for his sake was to be desired.' In the summer, Spitta, who had edited the Bach Edition and was a great friend, also died, and young Hermine Spiess. These losses conspired with his own feelings of withdrawal and isolation from the musical trends of the age to turn Brahms even more prematurely into an old man, although he could still be very jolly in the right company. George Henschel, visiting him in April of that year, had found him in a *lokale* surrounded by young contraltos and cracking broad jokes. When

Brahms in his study.

Henschel and his wife visited him at Karlsgasse 4 the following morning, he received them casually in an atmosphere of 'quiet inward happiness, contentment and ease' in his 'sunny, cosy room' filled with the smell of Viennese coffee brewed in his own coffee machine.

But that April, he had been subjected to one last irony: the Hamburg Philharmonic offered him the directorship he had longed for so many years before. Of course, it was now out of the question, and Brahms felt this bitterly. He wrote in his letter of refusal:

There are not many things that I have desired so long and so ardently at the time – that is, the right time. Many years had to pass before I could reconcile myself to the thought of being forced to tread other paths. Had things gone according to my wish, I might today be celebrating my jubilee with you, while you would be, as you are today, looking for a capable younger man. May you find him soon, and may he work in your interests with the same good will, the same modest degree of ability, and the same wholehearted zeal, as would have done yours very sincerely,

J. BRAHMS

Reflecting on these events in Ischl that summer, he composed his last sonatas, the two autumnal works for clarinet in F minor and E flat, Op.120, written once more with Mühlfeld in mind, although he also specified that they could be played on the violin or viola. During that summer, he also finished compiling his sets of German folk-songs with a group of forty-nine, the last of which, 'The moon steals up', had been used for a set of variations in his Piano Sonata in C major, Op.1, forty-one years before. Conscious of having completed a life's work well, he wrote to Clara:

It ought to represent the snake which bites its own tail, that is to say, to express symbolically that the tale is told, the circle closed . . . At sixty it is probably high time to stop.

And stop he did. For nearly two years, nothing more came from his pen. But the world would not let him become a recluse. In 1895 he found himself whisked off to attend music festivals dedicated to him. In Leipzig that February he took part in a three-day event which included his two piano concertos played by his latest protégé, the virtuoso Eugen d'Albert, and the two clarinet sonatas. Brahms and Mühlfeld were, as usual, the perfect musical partnership, and Brahms delighted in introducing the clarinettist as 'my prima donna' and 'Fraülein Klarinette' wherever they went.

After a quiet summer spent at Ischl, Brahms attended a festival at Meiningen in September which took von Bülow's dictum of Brahms being one of the three great 'Bs' of music as its theme. Bach and Beethoven were represented chiefly by the *St Matthew Passion* and the *Missa Solemnis*, and Brahms by his First

Symphony. Brahms enjoyed himself enormously; but, visiting Clara in Frankfurt on his way back to Vienna, he was distressed to find her very frail and ill.

In October he accepted an invitation to stay with Hegar in Zurich for a festival to celebrate the opening of its new concert hall. Widmann, who was present on the occasion, tells of the 'thundering applause' that greeted Brahms as he stepped onto the platform to conduct his *Triumphlied*. Beethoven's Choral Symphony took up the second half, and Brahms was flattered to see a portrait of himself on the ceiling next to those of Beethoven and other great masters of the classical school.

Typically, however, at the reception held in a wealthy music-lover's house afterwards, Brahms avoided the glittering guests and joined an improvised buffet on the stairs with his host's daughter and her young friends. There he sat 'laughing and joking' until past midnight.

In Leipzig the following January, George Henschel dined with Brahms and Grieg and found Brahms in the 'merriest of moods', consuming an 'astounding quantity of Munich beer'. He was next seen a few days later in Berlin, where he repeated the two-piano concerto bill with d'Albert and met the eighty-year-old German realist painter Adolph von Menzel, with whom he had struck up a friendship in Meiningen two years earlier, relishing many 'fine and enjoyable carousals'. Brahms wrote to Clara that he was attracted not only by his art, but by a life-style so akin to his: 'the only one of our famous men who lives in the most humble bourgeois circumstances.' Clara, although taking a polite interest in Brahms's enthusiasm for the artist, was too ill to write more than a postcard in reply.

In March, Grieg visited Brahms in Vienna and found him in such fine spirits that he invited him to Norway, whose mountains were 'the secret place where the treasure – your Fifth Symphony – lies hidden.' But Brahms would still have preferred Italy.

He wrote to Widmann that same month:

Do you not think of Italy for the spring, on account of your ears? On account of our legs, our eyes?

But Widmann was too ill to consider it, so the plans came to nothing.

Then, unexpectedly, in late March, Clara had a stroke. Brahms, bracing himself, wrote to her daughter, Marie:

If you think the worst is to be expected let me know so that I may come while those dear eyes are still open; for when they close, so much will end for me.

And to Joachim, he wrote:

When she has gone from us, will our faces not light up with joy at her memory, this glorious woman.

150

Music once more consoled him. In May he wrote the deeply personal *Four Serious Songs*, Op.121, for voice and piano, and began sketching an orchestral version that was never completed. The texts are from the Bible but, although strongly concerned with death, they rise to an affirmation of love at the close. He later explained their origin to Marie Schumann in a rare attempt to reveal his creative processes:

Deep in the heart of man something often whispers and stirs, quite unconsciously perhaps, which in time may ring out in the form of poetry or music.

Showing the songs to Kalbeck on 7 May, he described them grimly as his birthday present to himself. As she had always done, Clara sent him her birthday greeting, but it was no more than a few confused words scribbled from her sickbed. Then, on 20 March, she suffered another stroke and died.

Brahms was at Ischl when he received the news. He left for Frankfurt immediately, but was so agitated and distressed that he missed connections and took the wrong train. He travelled back and forth on the railway network for nearly two days before arriving in Frankfurt, only to find the funeral service over.

Clara was to be buried next to Robert Schumann in Bonn. Brahms rushed feverishly there on the next train but when he arrived, exhausted, he had only enough time to throw a handful of earth onto her coffin as it was lowered into the grave.

16 Into the Dark

The loss of Clara was a blow from which Brahms never recovered, 'Is life worth living when one is so alone?' he asked. After the funeral, he travelled briefly round the Rhineland, visiting old friends and conjuring up memories of his youth, before returning to Ischl, inwardly distraught. There, although he tried to resume his normal summer routine, he fell ill, almost psychosomatically, it is tempting to suggest; his complexion sallowed and his spirits depressed. Yet he still found time to think of Clara's daughters, Marie and Eugenie, to whom he wrote: 'I can think of no greater pleasure than to be able to serve, to advise or to help you in any way,' and later, when they offered him some memento of their mother: 'I must thank you, but . . . I want nothing. The smallest trifle would suffice me, but I possess the most beautiful of all!'

In this mood, he composed his last music: the Eleven Chorale Preludes, Op.122, for organ. The model is obviously Bach, and some may have been written earlier, but there is an unworldliness in all of them, and the last, entitled 'O World, I must depart from Thee', tells us everything about his state of mind.

As he showed no signs of recovery, he was finally persuaded to consult a local doctor. He diagnosed jaundice and prescribed Karlsbad salts as a cure, but a specialist from Vienna secretly shook his head. The salts had no effect, so Brahms was persuaded to visit Karlsbad itself and take the full cure. Hanslick, who knew the Bohemian spa town well, organised the journey with the help of Dr Fellinger, gave him introductions to friends of his in the town, and saw that he was comfortably lodged at an inn that was later to bear Brahms's name.

Outwardly, Brahms attempted to be cheerful and refused to hear anything bad about his complaint: 'I am grateful to my jaundice for having at last brought me to famous Karlsbad,' he wrote to Hanslick, and to Widmann he made light of it:

My indisposition need not make you in the least uneasy. It is quite a commonplace jaundice which unfortunately has the idiosyncrasy of not wanting to leave me.

But to Victor von Miller, he was less cheerful: 'Hanslick's fat friends here revolve amiably round me, though, recluse that I am, I do not welcome them very gratefully.'

Karlsbad did him no good; his condition deteriorated. A doctor in the town now diagnosed a 'serious swelling of the liver with

Brahms with friends, a photograph taken shortly before his death. Standing (left to right): Epstein, Mandyczewski, Hausmann. Seated (left to right): Fraulein Miller, Hanslick, Brahms, Frau Passini, Joachim.

complete blockage of the gall-ducts,' and on his return to Vienna the disease that had killed his father – cancer of the liver – was confirmed.

Brahms, who loathed ill-health in others, was told nothing of his real condition and attempted to ignore it in himself; but everyone else knew that the end was close. He became thin, haggard and self-absorbed, and would often leave company without saying a word. Knowing that there was little time left, he spent days sorting through old papers and manuscripts in his flat, destroying the vast majority of them.

He still attended concerts regularly. He heard a performance of the *Four Serious Songs* on 9 November, and when the Joachim Quartet arrived in the city to play his Second String Quintet on 2 January 1897, he was there to acknowledge the enthusiastic applause. His interest in Dvořák continued. On receiving his newly completed Cello Concerto in B minor, he played it through with Hausmann in his apartment. Deeply impressed, Brahms said afterwards, 'If I had known a concerto like that could have been written for the cello, I would have attempted one myself.' Later in the month, Dvořák visited Vienna for a performance of his *New World* Symphony, and went to see Brahms. Brahms, writing to the von Millers, attempted to keep cheerful:

Would you have any objection to my bringing him to see you? I will let him eat out of my little plate and drink out of my little glass and, as far as I know, he does not make speeches.

But even Dvořák could see that Brahms was dying and understood how bleak a prospect that was for such a man. 'Such a great soul,' he exclaimed, 'and yet he believes in *nothing*!'

He paid his last visit to a concert on 7 March when he heard his Fourth Symphony conducted by Richter at the Vienna

153

Philharmonic Society. When the last bars faded away, there was an ovation. Brahms stood up in his box, overcome with emotion, and gazed down on his beloved Viennese with tears in his eyes. When they saw his pale, shrunken figure, Hanslick reported:

A thrill of awe and painful sympathy ran through the whole assembly, a clear presentiment that they were greeting the suffering and beloved master for the last time in this hall.

His last public appearance was on 13 March when he attended a performance of Johann Strauss's operetta *The Goddess of Reason*, but he was too weak to hear it all, and had to leave half-way through.

When he could no longer walk in the public gardens to breathe the spring air that he loved, the Fabers, the von Millers and the Fellingers all pressed him to keep them company in their carriages as they drove round the Prater. The Duke of Meiningen sent him a crate of his favourite wine, and the Duchess sent a pair of warm slippers.

On 26 March, he retired to bed 'to rest a little'. He could not get up again. Frau Truxa attended to his every need. When she brought him a glass of the Duke of Meiningen's wine in the evening of 2 April, Brahms said to her, 'That tastes good, thank you,' then slept. Early the following morning, she entered the room again. Brahms woke, tried to speak, but could not. A tear formed in his eye and he died, peacefully, with hardly any pain.

★　　★　　★　　★

The man who loathed ceremony would not have approved of his own funeral, for nothing so splendid had been seen since the death of Beethoven. The streets and every vantage-point on the houses lining the route were filled with people, who watched a Spanish standard-bearer and torch-bearers accompany the hearse, followed by Dvořák, Alice Barbi, and dozens of Brahms's closest friends. So many flowers followed behind them that George Henschel, who was also present, called the procession 'a gigantic, moving garden'.

The cortège stopped briefly before the Vienna Philharmonic Society building, now covered in black cloth with blue flames flickering in suspended bowls. There, members of the *Singverein* performed Brahms's part-song *Fahr Wohl*. After a short service at the Dorotheergasse church, there was one last sung tribute at the graveside before Brahms was buried next to his revered predecessors, Beethoven and Schubert.

Hamburg, too, paid its respects and the flags on all the ships in its harbour were lowered to half-mast during the hour of the funeral.

He had led a full and active life, had been listed with the great, seen irrevocable changes in the workings of the world and the emergence of his own nation to undreamed-of heights of power and prestige. Everything pointed to happiness, but Brahms, for all his laughter, was not a happy man.

He had forfeited easy applause to avoid the pitfalls of his own inherently romantic nature and had adopted a lonely, traditional course, becoming a towering anachronism, like his great hero Bach. In his last years, he had moved into the position of revered monument but had seen the New German faction spawn the true music of the future: Richard Strauss and Gustav Mahler he knew and liked, although he could not warm to their music; Arnold Schoenberg, who was to revolutionise music entirely, often passed the elderly composer in the streets. None of this would have mattered if Brahms had been sure of himself, yet when the success that he had worked so hard to achieve came, he shunned it and longed for the bourgeois certainties of home and family that his single-minded creative urge could never accommodate. Much of the dissatisfaction that he nursed in his heart must be traced back to this paradox in himself.

Selected Bibliography

Dietrich, A. and Widmann, J. V. – *Recollections of Johannes Brahms*. London 1904.

Gal, Hans – *Johannes Brahms – His Work and Personality*. London, 1963.

Geiringer, Karl – *Brahms, His Life and Works*. London 1934.

Henschel, George – *Personal Recollections of Johannes Brahms*. Boston, 1907.

Kalbeck, M. – (Ed.) – *The Herzogenberg Correspondence*. London, 1909.

Latham, Peter – *Brahms*. (Master Musicians Series) London, 1948.

Litzmann, B. – (Ed.) – *The Letters of Clara Schumann and Johannes Brahms* (2 Vols). London, 1927.

May, Florence – *Life of Brahms* (2 Vols). London, 1905.

Niemann, W. – *Brahms*. London, 1929.

Schauffler, R. – *The Unknown Brahms*. New York, 1933.

Specht, R. – *Brahms*. London, 1930.

Brahms: Selective listing of works

Orchestral

Academic Festival Overture, Op. 80 21, 111, 113, 114

Concerto No. 1 for Piano and Orchestra, in D minor, Op. 15 41, 43, 45, 50, 51, 68, 149, 150

Concerto No. 2 for Piano and Orchestra in B flat, Op. 83 106, 116, 119, 122, 149, 150

Concerto for Violin, Cello and Orchestra in A minor, Op. 102 127-8, 109, 130, 134

Serenade No. 1 in D, Op. 11 41, 45, 5C, 57, 120

Serenade No. 2 in A, Op. 16 48, 50, 57, 68, 86, 120

Symphony No. 1 in C minor, Op. 68 52-3, 88, 89, 93, 94, 96, 97-9, 100, 102, 120, 149

Symphony No. 2 in D, Op. 73 100, 101-2, 103, 105, 106, 114, 119, 120, 131

Symphony No. 3 in F, Op. 90 119, 120-1, 122

Symphony No. 4 in E minor, Op. 98 121, 122-4

Tragic Overture, Op. 81 111, 113, 114

Variations on a Theme by Haydn (St Antony Chorale) Op. 56a 87, 86, 88

Chamber

Cello Sonata No. 1 in E minor, Op. 38 66

Cello Sonata No. 2 in F, Op. 99 124, 127, 153-4

Clarinet Quintet in B minor, Op. 115 143, 145

Clarinet Sonata No. 1 in F minor, Op. 120a 149

Clarinet Sonata No. 2 in E flat, Op. 120b 149

Clarinet Trio in A minor, Op. 114 143

Horn Trio in E flat, Op. 40 66, 68

Piano Quartet No. 1 in G minor, Op. 25 48, 56

Piano Quartet No. 2 in A, Op. 25 51, 56

Piano Quartet No. 3 in C minor, Op. 60 93

Piano Quintet in F minor, Op. 34a 52, 64, 86

Piano Trio No. 1 in B, Op. 8 30, 31, 137

Piano Trio No. 2 in C, Op. 87 112, 113, 118

Piano Trio No. 3 in C minor, Op. 101 124

Piano Trio in A (attrib. Brahms 1938) 28

Scherzo from the FAE Violin Sonata 26

String Quartet No. 1 in C minor, Op. 51 No. 1 68, 86, 87

String Quartet No. 2 in A minor, Op. 51 No. 2 86, 87

String Quartet No. 3 in B flat, Op. 67 93, 94

String Quintet No. 1 in F, Op. 88 118

String Quintet No. 2 in G, Op. 111 141, 153

String Sextet No. 1 in B flat, Op. 18 48, 52, 61, 86

String Sextet No. 2 in G Op. 36 (Agathe) 48, 52

Violin Sonata No. 1 in G, Op. 78 106, 108

Violin Sonata No. 2 in A, Op. 100 124, 127

Violin Sonata No. 3 in D minor, Op. 108 133, 134

Piano

Fantasy on a Favourite Waltz 15

Fifty-one Didactic Exercises 112

Four Ballades, Op. 10 33

Four Pieces, Op. 119 147

Hungarian Dances (First Set) 69, 139

Hungarian Dances (Second Set) 69

Intermezzi and Capriccii, Op. 76 105

Piano Sonata No. 1 in C, Op. 1 15, 18, 24, 27, 140, 149

Piano Sonata No. 2 in F sharp minor, Op. 2 15, 18, 27, 140

Piano Sonata No. 3 in F minor, Op. 5 21, 29, 57, 140

Scherzo in E flat minor, Op. 4 15, 18, 20, 25, 27

Six Fantaisies, Op. 116 144

Six Pieces, Op. 118 147

Sonata for Two Pianos in F minor, Op. 34b 52, 64

Three Intermezzi, Op. 117 144

Two Rhapsodies, Op. 79 108

Variations and Fugue on a Theme by Handel, Op. 24 51-2, 56, 61, 69

Variations on a Hungarian Theme, Op.21 33

Variations on a Theme by Haydn (St Anthony Variations) Op. 56b 86

Variations on a Theme by Paganini (Two Books), Op. 35 55, 69

Index

Illustrations are indicated in bold type

159

160